LITURGIES FOR RESISTING EMPIRE

LITURGIES FOR RESISTING EMPIRE

Seeking Community, Belonging, and Peace
in a Dehumanizing World

KAT ARMAS

 BrazosPress
a division of Baker Publishing Group
Grand Rapids, Michigan

© 2025 by Kat Armas

Published by Brazos Press
a division of Baker Publishing Group
Grand Rapids, Michigan
BrazosPress.com

Library of Congress Cataloging-in-Publication Data
Names: Armas, Kat, 1989– author
Title: Liturgies for resisting empire : seeking community, belonging, and peace in a dehumanizing world / Kat Armas.
Description: Grand Rapids, Michigan : Brazos Press, a division of Baker Publishing Group, [2025] | Includes bibliographical references.
Identifiers: LCCN 2025015148 | ISBN 9781587436499 paperback | ISBN 9781493450268 ebook
Subjects: LCSH: Communities—Religious aspects—Christianity | Peace—Religious aspects—Christianity | Liberty—Religious aspects—Christianity
Classification: LCC BV625 .A753 2025 | DDC 261—dc23/eng/20250627
LC record available at https://lccn.loc.gov/2025015148

Cover design by Chris Tobias / Tobias Design, Inc.

The author is represented by the literary agency of Gardner Literary Agency, LLC.

Baker Publishing Group publications use paper produced from sustainable forestry practices and postconsumer waste whenever possible.

25 26 27 28 29 30 31   7 6 5 4 3 2 1

This one's for you, T.
You are every word in these pages, breathing and alive.
Somehow you carry the weight of them all,
and still you make the load feel light.
I am more human,
more whole,
because of you.

Contents

Preface

This book lived many lives before finding its way into your hands. The idea first took root in me during Advent of 2021, when I first became a mother. It began to take a clear shape a year and a half later, in the summer of 2023. By this point, I had spent years studying empire and postcolonial theology in seminary and divinity school, but something in me longed to hear these conversations break free from the academy. I wanted to see them reflected in the rhythms of ordinary life. Many of us hunger for an honest reckoning with empire and the ways it has crept into our bones, shaping how we live, love, and belong.

At times, this work felt impossibly beyond me. But creativity is a relentless force; it pursues you until you surrender—and so I wrote. Then, in October of 2023, the devastation in Gaza came crashing into my consciousness. I couldn't write about empire without holding this in my hands, without attempting to understand its histories, its griefs, its complexities. So I read and listened and learned. Empire demands we pay attention to the stories it has fractured.

While writing, I found myself navigating the sacred thresholds of motherhood again. Carrying my second child, a son, felt different. Raising my daughter had been a work of decolonization. I was parenting her under the shadow of colonialism, patriarchy, and capitalism, systems that have long weighed most heavily on women. But a son? He demanded a new kind of reckoning, a stripping away of the systems I'd inherited so I could mother him with both integrity and tenderness. I wrote for her, and now I was writing for him too.

This book was born alongside a life lived in all its fullness: through pregnancy and birth, through sleepless nights and post-partum recovery. I wrote amid the clamor of a toddler's laughter, the tender work of tending a farm, the grief of family loss, and the quiet joy of nurturing an animal back to health. I wrote through my friends' miscarriages, some births, a presidential election, and the raw ache of being human. This is the nature of life—to write, to live, and to wrestle with what it means to be fully alive in the midst of life's fiercest realities. This is also what it means to resist empire.

And liturgies?

Liturgy finds its origin in the Greek words for "people" and "work." It is the labor of a community, alongside the prayers, meditations, and rituals that shape us as we gather. Empire, with its hunger for domination, division, and isolation trembles at this. It fears our togetherness, our longing for belonging. And so we must resist the forces of individualism and discord that threaten to unravel us. This resistance does not deny the necessity of solitude. It is in the quiet exploration of our inner landscapes that healing begins, not just for ourselves but for the collective whole.

Each chapter of this book begins with an invocation, calling on the sacred to guide and bless us. As we do this, we also acknowledge ancestors who have lived under empires past. Their stories linger, reminding us of the wisdom in their struggle. From there, you'll find parables or fables from non-Western cultures, ways of knowing that empire has often tried to erase. These stories hold lessons for us and invite us to sit with truths that can't always be intellectualized. Then each chapter unveils a defining characteristic or insidious "lie" of empire—a pattern woven into the fabric of the world as we know it. These patterns are ways of being we must confront and reject, making room instead for new rhythms of living that nurture freedom, truth, and collective flourishing. Each chapter then closes with a prayer of resistance and a benediction, offering a space to exhale, to ground the weight of what you've read in something sacred.

Whether you read alone or with a community, let these prayers and reflections guide you not toward easy answers but toward the sacred work of wrestling, confessing, and dreaming of something freer. There is no right way to do this work, only the honest way. Let us begin.

A Liturgy for Resisting Empire

Invocation

God Who Dwells on the Margins, where power does not dare to look, we call upon you, the sacred who lives in whispers and shadows—in the quiet, where words are not rushed, where power has no place to hide. Let us be grounded in your mystery, for you are more than nation, more than law or hierarchy. You are the hidden strength in the fragile and the small. We call upon you, Spirit of the oppressed and the silenced, help us to let go of all the small tyrannies within: the worry, the fear, the need for control. Here, we choose to resist the powers that would divide us, exploit us, or convince us to believe in our own isolation.

May we find courage in your presence, and may we resist the voices that seek to dominate our souls.

Prayer of Confession: Acknowledging Our Complicity

God of Liberation,
We confess the ways we have been entangled in the workings of empire. How some of us may have sought comfort at the expense of others' dignity. Or stayed silent in the presence of suffering,

sought safety over solidarity, accepted dominance over humility. Let us release the ways we have used our own power as empire would, and let us begin again, in truth and in courage.

Hold us in your mercy when we've upheld systems of injustice or been crushed by them. Help us to see clearly, to name truthfully, and to resist humbly. Turn us toward life that does not dominate but sustains, that does not exploit but nourishes. Open our hands to surrender the power that harms and to tend the wounds it leaves behind.

Guide us to honor each life as a sanctuary of the sacred.

Readings from Sacred Texts

Isn't this the fast I choose:
 releasing wicked restraints, untying the ropes of a yoke,
 setting free the mistreated,
 and breaking every yoke?
Isn't it sharing your bread with the hungry
 and bringing the homeless poor into your house,
 covering the naked when you see them,
 and not hiding from your own family?

—Isaiah 58:6–7

Jesus . . . said, "You know that those who rule the Gentiles show off their authority over them and their high-ranking officials order them around. But that's not the way it will be with you. Whoever wants to be great among you will be your servant."

—Matthew 20:25–26

Prayer of Resistance

O God, we resist the temptations of empire: control, comfort, and apathy.

Help us walk in a way that honors your vision of wholeness and liberation.

We choose love that frees, justice that restores, and peace that is born of truth.

When we fail to see your image in the oppressed and the marginalized, open our eyes, O God. Make us defenders of dignity. Show us the way of humility.

Let us live lives that bear witness to a kingdom that is not of domination but of deep communion. Teach us to honor your image in ourselves and one another.

Amen.

Benediction

May God strengthen our hearts to confront injustice, knowing that resistance is not simply a cry or an act but a way of being. May we have courage to face the world unbowed by power, unafraid of truth. And may we go with a spirit of compassion and humility, knowing that God walks with the oppressed and dwells among the disinherited.

Amen.

CHAPTER 1

Rejecting Empire, Embracing Joy

Invocation

Divine Liberation, we acknowledge our place in a world marked by systems of exploitation. Let us open our hearts to how these systems live and move through us. May we move toward freedom, together.

We are here to listen, to learn, and to act with compassion and love.

Reflection

The Quechua people tell a story about a hummingbird:

There was a time when the Great Forest caught fire. The flames roared and the smoke billowed, and all the animals fled in fear. Gathering at the edge of the forest, they watched as their home burned and burned.

"What can I do?" cried Buck.

"This fire is so big, and I am so small!" howled Fox.

Among them hovered a tiny hummingbird, her beak the size of a honeybee. She flew to a nearby stream, picked up a single drop of water, and flew back, dropping it into the fire. She made her way back and forth from the stream to the flames, carrying one drop at a time. Over and over.

The other animals watched, confused. Finally, Bear asked her, "Little Hummingbird, what are you doing?"

The hummingbird looked at the animals and said, "I am doing what I can."

Those who have ears let them hear.

I wake earlier than I intend, the first notes of birdsong filtering through the crack in the window, the soft light of dawn just beginning to trace its way across my room. I exhale slowly, releasing a small sigh of gratitude for this new day.

Then the light of my phone pulls me from this quiet place. A headline. Another tragedy. More innocent lives stolen, so many of them women and children. It's been two hundred days now.

Yesterday, I read about a massacre that took place while people were in line, waiting for bread. I paused, heart heavy, before moving into the kitchen to make myself something to eat. Later, I saw an image of a family buried in rubble, a child's face twisted in terror. I winced, caught my breath, and then slipped under the covers with my own family to read my child a bedtime story. I kissed her goodnight.

There are no words, none, for the collective pain we're bearing. For the bodies, souls, and lives that are still being slaughtered.

It's too much. It's all too much.

As I write these words, over 150 Israeli hostages remain missing, kidnapped on October 7, 2023, by Hamas, an armed Palestinian group whose attack—one that killed over 1,200 innocent people—came after decades of Israeli occupation and oppression. In response, the Israeli government launched an assault so devastating that tens of thousands of Palestinians have been killed and countless others injured or displaced. Hospitals bombed, food and water cut off—human rights violations no one can deny.

Thanks to social media, we didn't just hear about the atrocities happening in Gaza; we saw them unfold in real time, on the screens in our hands, on waking, as we went about our days, when we tried to close our eyes and rest. Images of children, lifeless, cradled in the arms of their caregivers, flooded our feeds.

You might wonder why I chose to start this book with this brutality. Because when the earth groans so must we. Because speaking of peace and justice in a fractured world requires that we acknowledge the brokenness and the violence that continue to spread unchecked.

Confronting the Theology of Empire

On Christmas Eve 2023, Palestinian pastor Munther Isaac stood in Bethlehem and spoke of a theology that disguises itself as divine but is far from it. He said:

> Here we confront the theology of empire. A disguise for superiority, supremacy, "chosenness," and entitlement. It is sometimes given a nice cover using words like *mission* and *evangelism*, fulfillment of prophecy, and spreading freedom and liberty. The theology of the empire becomes a powerful tool to mask oppression under the cloak of divine sanction. It speaks of land without people. It divides people into "us" and "them." It dehumanizes and demonizes the concept of land without people even when they know the land has people.[1]

Isaac's words carry the weight of a history in which land, bodies, and dignity have been claimed in the name of power. It's a history of walls and checkpoints, of lives hemmed in by curfews, raids, and the constant threat of violence. It's a history of settlers seizing land with impunity, leaving Palestinians without recourse to justice. This history stretches back to British imperial rule, the rise of Zionism, and Israel's founding in 1948, which created a Jewish state and led to the violent expulsion and displacement of hundreds of thousands of Palestinians.

Isaac's words on Christmas Eve have stayed with me. In them, I hear the heart of why this all matters. Why the tangled histories of displacement matter. Why the land matters. Why this war—this genocide—happening, for many of us, on the other side of the world, matters. Because it is not just about land or politics. It is about bodies. Children dying over imperial interests. And it's about a theology of empire, one so deeply embedded in our faith and our world that we often don't see it for what it is. It's a way of thinking that has shaped us, shaped how we see each other, and shaped how we understand divinity. I wonder sometimes if it's even possible to disentangle ourselves from its grip.

This book is my attempt to begin that disentangling. I won't claim that these pages hold all the answers or that they will resolve the complexities of colonized faith. Many have written in detail about the histories of empire and colonization; this is not that kind of book. Instead, I hope to offer a wider view, a look at how empire has seeped into our imagination and our theology. I hope my words can be like the tweezers, the alcohol, the balm that might start to lift the empire's imprint from our skin. It will take a lifetime to heal from its sting, but perhaps this can be a beginning.

―――――

I currently live in middle Tennessee, a land that isn't the start of my story but where I find myself being molded by the rhythm of a place and what it reveals about the world around me. I am in the United States, a country that claims my birthright but is not the home of my ancestors, whose stories stretch across shores and generations far beyond its borders. This is the tension I carry, the complexity that shapes my identity and my faith. My story is not just my own; it is braided with the story of empire. And so is yours.

Though I sit far from the soil of Israel and Palestine, the suffering of the people there is not distant from me. We are all bound together, even if we don't always sense it. Our shared humanity is in the air we breathe, the earth we walk upon, the moon we gaze at. It's the same moon, the same air, the same ground—no matter where our feet or hearts land. Our connection runs deeper than the physical, though. There's a tether in our psyches, a thread that links our fears, desires, and longings. Every human, across every border, wants safety, love, and belonging. None of us desires suffering, for ourselves or for those we hold close.

Yet empire weaves our stories into its grand narrative, forcing us into entanglements we don't always see. The modern world is shaped by individual societies that are deeply intertwined within a global economic system. European colonialism played a pivotal role in building this interconnected global network, leading to the rise of capitalism and globalization and a world increasingly connected through economic exchange. The expansion of markets has bound us, as individuals and societies, into a vast web of commercial interactions involving goods, money, capital, and labor.[2]

This global structure, often referred to as a "world system," explains why many hold the United States partly responsible for the deaths in Gaza. Societies are inextricably linked together as part of a broader social network, and their actions and policies impact and shape one another—often within unequal political and economic relationships.[3] These unequal affiliations, whether acknowledged or not, affect each one of us.

The capitalist world economy influences our relationship to time, our bodies, our families, and our sense of purpose. It shapes our priorities, our responsibilities, and how we understand ourselves and others. My hope is that this book will help illuminate how this happened and how we can foster new, life-giving ways of belonging to each other in a world marked by division, discord, and individualism. Empire, after all, is not a relic of the past. It's alive, entrenched in our daily rhythms. This was true for the early followers of Jesus under Roman rule, and it is true for us today. As Palestinian scholar Edward Said notes, empire isn't just soldiers and weapons; it's ideas, attitudes, practices, and stories.[4] It's a way of imagining the world.

I wrote this book to uncover the imperial ideologies woven into our everyday lives—whether we are raising children, shopping, working, vacationing, or enjoying a meal with friends. More specifically, I wrote it to uncover the imperial ideologies woven into our spirituality, our churches, our study of the Bible. Understanding these ideologies is essential to understanding ourselves, our world, and our faith—and to imagining new ways of being and belonging.

———————

Weeks after October 7, 2023, Jewish American journalist Ezra Klein launched a series of podcast episodes centered on Israel and Palestine. He interviewed Sharon Brous, the senior rabbi of a Los Angeles synagogue. During their conversation, Klein pressed Rabbi Brous on a statement she had made claiming that the actions of the increasingly right-wing government in Israel were "un-Jewish." He highlighted the contradiction: "It's the most observant, the most religious Israelis who are the most comfortable turning Israel into this entity that you and I fear. They view the religion we share, though understood differently, as a call for conquering biblical lands." He then posed a piercing question: "You're a rabbi. . . . What are you reading differently than these . . . very learned rabbis?"[5]

As someone who started my Protestant faith journey in white evangelical spaces, I immediately connected with Klein's question. In more recent years, I've been drawn to the ways people can engage the same sacred texts yet arrive at radically different understandings. This is what the work of theology involves:

discerning meaning from the margins and the center, and navigating the unspoken space between.

Rabbi Brous responded by noting that every person is engaging in an act of interpretation. I nodded. *Yes, this is true.* She explained that as a rabbi and interpreter she chooses to start with Genesis, where it says that all humans are made in the image of God. *A strong foundation*, I thought. She continued by grounding her faith in the exodus story, a narrative of an enslaved people walking from cruelty toward a promised land to build a just society. For her, the exodus is a call to moral action, a call to extend hospitality to the stranger because you were strangers (see Lev. 19:34). "That is the source of my Jewish faith," she said. "Maybe I'm reading our tradition wrong, and maybe those extremist, messianic figures deep in the West Bank who are teaching soldiers that they need to wipe out the enemy, maybe are right and I'm wrong."[6]

The biblical story of Israel is indeed one of exile, in which God's people are called to welcome the stranger and avoid oppressing others as they themselves were oppressed. This is a central biblical command. When we read this, it becomes clear that occupying a land, limiting people's access to basic resources, and perpetuating injustice don't align with the biblical message. However, there's another truth I can't ignore. While I agree with Rabbi Brous's interpretation of Israel's story, something still unsettles me.

The truth is that extremists in Israel may not be acting "unbiblically" in the way progressive leaders often claim. In fact, high-ranking Israeli officials can cite Scripture to justify their brutal actions. The Bible, at face value, contains commands from God to destroy entire populations, to leave no survivors (Deut. 20:16–17). For many of us, this feels unnerving, so we try to explain it away. I know I have in the past. But my convictions as a postcolonial scholar won't allow me to do so anymore. To ignore these difficult texts or pretend they haven't shaped the lived experiences of millions—from Palestinians in Gaza to

Native Americans on US soil—is to fail to take both the Bible and my faith seriously.

This is because the Bible is not merely an artifact of history but a living text that influences present-day decisions. If it is meant to truly liberate, then we must reckon with it, resisting the urge to rescue or sanitize it for the sake of our discomfort. Doing so allows the Bible to remain an unsafe text for many people. Only by acknowledging the Bible's complicity in violent ideologies and actions can we begin the work of addressing the injustices woven into its pages.

This is why I appreciate the work of postcolonialism, because it exposes the ambivalences, contradictions, and paradoxes in Scripture. It challenges us to become more critical, nuanced thinkers so that we live out "on earth as it is in heaven," making "the least of these" our foremost concern.[7] It teaches us to hold the complexity of survival with tenderness for the sake of our shared liberation.

This book, then, is not about defending or sugarcoating the Bible; it is about letting it be what it is. I have no interest in upholding the Western binaries that reduce the world's complexity to simple answers. Instead, I want to trace how the Bible interacts with both the structural and relational realities of those living under empire and the lasting impact of its power.[8]

My hope is that these pages will challenge you to dwell in the both/and of the Bible, exploring how its stories wrestle with empire in both unsettling and comforting ways that either deny or affirm our biases and beliefs.

———

Empires have always created their own ideologies in order to justify domination and control. These beliefs become systems of oppression over people and land alike.[9] And in their wake, we are left with existential questions about identity and belonging that pierce the deepest parts of our being. Questions like "Who is my neighbor?" (Luke 10:29) and "My God, my God, why have you left me?" (Matt. 27:46). The answers to these questions are flesh and blood. They not only shape who we are, rippling through our lives, but also steer the course of history, which unfolds through the telling of stories. Stories are never innocent, never impartial. They carry the weight of perspective, ideology, and cultural values. Our stories are no exception. When we retell them, we do so from the lens of who we are today, with the knowledge and experience we hold in the moment. This means that our understanding of the past is colored by where we currently stand geographically, politically, and socially. We can never truly be objective, neutral observers.[10] Because of this, there is no pure, unfiltered story; there's only the truth we carry now. As I recall episodes from my childhood, I recognize the way my understanding of them shifts with time, with healing, with the slow revelation of what it means to belong to a family or a people. Each retelling is an act of interpretation, and in that act there is power.

To interpret our own stories is to reclaim something sacred, to perform an act of resistance. The interpreter becomes the storyteller, the one who shapes their own history. But to be colonized is to be stripped of that power; it is to be erased from one's own story. This is part of empire's violence: seizing control of interpretation, rewriting the past to impose its own narrative on people's lives, land, and ancestors.

Biblical scholars have played a part in this erasure, reducing a text born in the heart of political and imperial struggle—a text that addresses economic, religious, and historical realities—to mere dogma. In doing so, they have ignored the imperial context and colonial dynamics that shaped the Bible's origins, pretending they were never there.[11] But the Bible in its entirety tells the story of empires—from Egypt to Assyria, Babylon, Persia, and Rome.

Exodus recounts the story of a people plucked from the grip of Egypt's clenched fist. The story of the Israelites is a story of what it means to unlearn the rhythms of empire and learn how to walk as a people whose life and identity are free from oppression.

As we move through the Hebrew scriptures, we hear the echoes of empire in so many places: from the prayers whispered in desperation to the defiant prophecies and the words of warning not to become the very thing they fled. The story of God's people—from Moses to Daniel to Esther—is a story of empire. Every book of the Bible wrestles with what it means to exist within a context of imperial rule.

And yet, some treat the Bible as if it's somehow untouched by politics, as if it's concerned with only the spiritual and not these gritty realities. Most interpreters would have us believe that Jesus's followers, for example, quietly accepted Roman authority and respected Rome's rulers unless they were forced to choose between Christ and Caesar.[12] But as we will see, this is far from the truth. Instead, many of the Bible's letters and narratives are those of everyday people contending with, responding to, and critiquing empire in their day-to-day lives.

What Do We Mean by Empire, Anyway?

I was talking with friends and fellow seminary graduates around the time this book started to take form. When I shared my idea, their eyes lit up. They told me that just weeks earlier their church group had spent hours wrestling with this very topic: empire. They wanted to understand how it affects their lives but were having trouble doing so.

Hearing this affirmed two things I already sensed. First, to have meaningful conversations, we need to know what we're talking about. I admire that church group for doing the hard work of coming together to discuss and to search for common ground. Isn't this what we're called to do as people of faith and as a human community? To listen deeply, to wrestle with ideas together, to learn from one another, to disagree and grow? To be open to changing our minds? These should be our goals, not just for ourselves but for the sake of those journeying alongside us.

Second, the notion of empire can feel overwhelming and elusive. What exactly do we mean when we say "empire"? And what does our faith have to do with it? What role does the Bible play? These questions don't come with simple answers.

Perhaps this is why the concept is so challenging to grasp and even define, because it deals not only with political realities but with emotional ones. Empire isn't an abstract idea; it involves real, living beings who embody multiple identities and contradictions, and who carry complex stories of oppression and survival, trauma and resilience. Untangling something this vast will inevitably leave things unsaid or unexplored.

Empires have existed as long as human history itself, taking different shapes in different times. Many ancient political systems— from the Akkadians to the early states of India and China—are often described as empires. Some were land-based, like the Assyrians, the Greeks, and the Persians, while others built their power across the seas, like the Spanish, the French, and the British. Later centuries would bring medieval and modern empires such as the Ottoman, Byzantine, and Russian. And of course there was the Roman Empire, which I will often refer to because of how deeply it shaped the world we live in today. Roman imperialism created a template for later empires, serving as both a model and a warning. For Christians, it provides the context for the story of the church recounted in the New Testament.

Because I'm US American with Caribbean roots, European colonialism and American imperialism have left their mark on my story and the story of my ancestors. These are the empires that dominate contemporary conversations, and they will be central to what I explore here. But it's important to understand the impact of ancient empires, because there are threads we can trace through them all—threads of power and domination, homogeneity and hierarchy, conquest and violence. These patterns, though varied, stretch across time, shaping how we understand the world and our place in it.

For many, empire is the villain—the tyrant, the oppressor, the force of destruction. But for those who've benefited from its rule, empire hasn't always been seen this way. History has often cast empire as heroic, a symbol of greatness. Adventurers risked their lives in its name, driven by a sense of duty. Rome, Britain, and others upheld empire as something noble, and even those crushed beneath its weight sometimes longed for the power it promised. This is the seduction of empire: Power can feel impossible to resist.

It's no surprise, then, that when Israel escaped Egypt, God's first instruction was clear: *Do not oppress the foreigner* (Exod. 22:21). They knew empire's cruelty, suffered as outsiders under Egyptian rule. And yet power's appeal is so great that even the oppressed can turn into oppressors when the balance shifts.

To complicate matters, the same people can be both colonizers and colonized, imperialists and victims, all at once. White settlers on Turtle Island (North America) devastated Indigenous nations and enslaved African peoples, yet they also saw themselves as victims of the British monarchy, leading the world's first anticolonial revolution. In Australia, white settlers fought for independence from Britain even as they seized and subjugated Aboriginal lands.[13] These tensions reveal the tangled nature of empire: its contradictions, its ambiguity, its ability to both wound and justify itself in the same breath.

At its core, empire is about the relationship between a dominant, ruling state and a less powerful one. The word originates from the Latin *imperium*, meaning "dominion, sovereignty, power, or rule," and originally described a political system governed by an emperor.[14] As empire grew, particularly under Rome, it expanded to signify something larger, an ambition not just to hold power but to stretch that power across distant lands and over its inhabitants. Empire is fundamentally about the extension of control, whether through direct domination or subtle influence. And in that expansion, something essential is always sacrificed.

Imperialism differs from empire in that it's less about the physical empire itself and more about the spirit of conquest behind it.

Those driven by an imperial mentality believe they are entitled to not only occupy lands that aren't theirs but also to impose their language and their economic and political systems on the people who inhabit those lands. Consider the audacity of a declaration like Donald Trump's in the beginning of his second term: "The U.S. will take over the Gaza Strip and we will do a good job with it, too. . . . I do see a long-term ownership position."[15]

Imperialists see the world as something to be conquered. Imperialism, therefore, fosters hierarchies by suppressing local traditions and cultures in favor of a narrow set of universal standards that benefit those in power.[16] At its core, imperialism captures the exhilaration of expansion and the insatiable hunger for control.[17]

Today, we see imperialism less in the overt colonization of land and more in the influence of Western corporations, the way brands like Coca-Cola, Disney, McDonald's, and Amazon have knit themselves into the fabric of nations, dictating not just what people consume but what they value. In the shadow of the Cold War, critics began to see US foreign policy as imperialism itself, woven from threads of military force, economic coercion, and cultural dominance, stretching into places like Central America and beyond.

When we speak of imperialism today, we often think of power that is Western, capitalist, and white. Though it may not resemble colonialist rule of the nineteenth and twentieth centuries, it operates with the same intent: control, exploitation, and the readiness to use military power to protect its interests.[18]

Untangling from Empire's Narratives

I've laid out a few key terms to set the foundation for exploring how these ideologies shape our minds and our theologies. I define other terms in later chapters, but I want to be clear that my attempt at tackling these concepts is not meant to be definitive. In fact, rarely do people, scholars, or even experts fully agree on the exact meanings of these terms. Perhaps they never will, as the subject of empire stirs both political passions and deep emotions. These words and their meanings are living, layered, and complex—just like empire's legacies. Wherever we come from, whatever faith or culture we claim, empire's reach has touched our lives in ways we are still learning to name.

I write this as a woman shaped by two worlds. I am a Western-educated, Cuban American raised in Miami's Cuban exile community. My family arrived as refugees in the heat of the Cold War—a period of political, economic, and ideological rivalry between the United States and the Soviet Union. The Cuban Revolution of 1959 led by Fidel Castro was the reason for our migration, but its roots run deeper, tangled in the shadow of empire. For many in my community, the US empire became a kind of savior, the antidote to Castro's rule. Yet it's impossible to ignore how that same power set the stage for the revolution through economic exploitation, support of corrupt regimes, and a steady erosion of Cuban sovereignty. But that's the cunning of empire: It creates the very vulnerability it later claims to rescue you from. And in moments of desperation, it can be hard to see the deception. This dynamic is central to my personal story and the broader story of domination and control. Throughout history, empire has been skilled at selling us the narratives it wants us to believe—offering a false sense of security or salvation—but we are not bound to accept them. We have the power to break free and find new ways of being and belonging. The question we must ask is, how do we untangle ourselves from these narratives? And when we do, what kind of freedom awaits us?

I wrestle with these questions for the sake of our shared humanity. The paradox of being human is that we learn to find hope and meaning in a world scarred by pain and brokenness. We fight for our dignity and joy within systems designed to exploit us. We heal our individual wounds, understanding that doing so ripples out toward the healing of the whole. Why? Because at the heart of the human experience is the longing to belong. This is a thread woven throughout the Bible. Its pages tell of people grappling with what it means to belong to God and to one another within systems of oppression marked by hierarchy and dominance, scarcity and hustle, exclusion and violence.

I think of the day Jesus sat in a boat, teaching the crowds on the shore. When he said, "The kingdom of God is . . ." they leaned in, bracing for words about men and armies, kings and dominion. They expected images of power, grandeur, and conquest. But Jesus, with gentle subversion, spoke instead of a woman. A woman who took a little yeast, hid it in dough, and watched it rise into enough bread to nourish a whole community.

This kingdom does not arrive with spectacle or force; it moves in unseen, quiet abundance through the ordinary. It breaks apart the illusions of power. It shatters our expectations.

So how do we pursue hope, joy, and liberation alongside our neighbors and the divine while living in systems designed to manufacture despair? How do we move toward justice when empire demands our exhaustion, when scarcity is woven into the fabric of our world? How do we resist oppression without becoming consumed by it? These are the sacred questions we carry on this journey—not for easy answers, but for the fullness of life itself.

I invite you to join me in this exploration, to examine our past and reclaim our present so that we can build a more just future. Like the work of the hummingbird in the Great Forest fire, our efforts may feel like one small drop at a time. But this is the work of decolonizing. This is what healing looks like: Doing what we can, with what we have, in the capacity we're given.

Prayer of Resistance

God of Liberation,

We confess the ways fatigue and fear prevent us from resisting empire fully. Allow us to receive forgiveness like a balm—a sacred release from guilt so that we may be empowered to take action.

We untether ourselves from empire's grasp and step into a life of integrity and freedom.

Benediction

May the courage within us rise like a quiet flame, small yet steady. Let the spirit of the hummingbird—a creature so delicate yet relentless, its wings creating ripples in the air—guide us. What we do may seem small, but even the smallest motions can shift the tide.
Amen.

CHAPTER 2

Rejecting Lies, Embracing Reality

Invocation

Wellspring of Truth, may your wild edges unravel what we thought we knew. Where beauty and terror breathe as one, you invite us to stay and not turn away, to witness your mystery in all that is both glorious and undone.

We reject the lies we are sold about ourselves and the world. We reclaim the truth that has been buried beneath their weight.

Reflection

Danish author Hans Christian Andersen told a story about an emperor:

Once there was an emperor obsessed with fine clothes. Two swindlers came to his court, claiming they could weave a fabric so exquisite that it would be invisible to anyone who was foolish. Intrigued, the emperor paid them handsomely to create an outfit from this magical fabric. The weavers worked at empty looms, pretending to weave. When the emperor's officials went to check on the progress, they saw nothing but feared admitting it, thinking doing so would reveal their incompetence. So they praised the invisible fabric. The emperor, also seeing nothing, went along with the deception to avoid looking foolish.

The emperor decided to wear the "clothes" in a grand parade. As he walked through the streets, no one in the crowd dared admit they saw nothing. Then a child in the crowd, unburdened by fear or pride, shouted, "But he's not wearing anything at all!" The crowd murmured in agreement, and soon everyone saw the truth. Embarrassed but too proud to stop, the emperor continued his parade, knowing he had been exposed.

Those who have ears let them hear.

The line snaked around the building, bodies fidgeting in the humid air. Some held signs; others wore T-shirts with Bible verses plastered across the back like shields. My phone buzzed. It was a Friday night, and my friends were headed to the bar. "I'm at a conference," I texted back. "I'll meet up later." They laughed. "Of course you are." No surprise there. Those who knew me understood this about me—that I'd find myself at an evangelical conference, of all places, alone. Just for the experience.

The energy in the crowd was palpable, a hum of anticipation hanging in the air. My last encounter with anything like this had been at a school mass the Friday before graduation. Seniors, crammed into the gym under basketball hoops, receiving the Eucharist while passing notes across the bleachers. We were buzzing too, but it was more about relief that school was almost over than about anything holy.

This felt different.

When the doors opened, the crowd surged forward, bodies pressing together like a tsunami. I got swept up in the flood and found myself near the front. The name *Jesus* flashed on a massive screen, and suddenly I felt like I had entered a new world. Who were these people, so young and stylish, vibrating with urgency? The auditorium went dark, and the first strum of the guitar sent a ripple through the crowd. Hands shot up in the air as if they were grasping for something I couldn't yet see.

Men with long hair and beards took the stage. I had never heard of Hillsong, but they seemed to be important. The word *Jesus* became a chant, echoing through the room. I didn't know what was happening, but I felt it. The lights, the sound, and the emotion were overwhelming—electric. This was church? I didn't understand it, but I was drawn in, caught up in the spectacle of it all.

Speaker after speaker took the stage, each more fervent than the last. "Give everything to Jesus," they pleaded, and by the end of the service, I was ready to. Of course, I'd give up anything for *this*.

I didn't meet my friends at the bar that night. Instead, by the time the night was over, I had decided to "give my life to Jesus." I wasn't entirely sure what that phrase meant, as I believed I already knew Jesus from my years in Catholicism, but I was sure of one thing: I had to go back the next day to feel it all again.

On the last night of the conference, something happened. As I walked out of the final worship session, I heard someone call my name. I turned, confused. It was a family member I hadn't spoken to in years. After a brief chat, they invited me to their megachurch. Days later, I arrived there and didn't look back.

This world brought with it an unexpected sense of security. Suddenly, I felt like I was a part of something, surrounded by people who shared not just my faith but, soon, my values. There's a kind of comfort that comes from knowing you're in the right, that your salvation is secure. Maybe it's this feeling of belonging that many seek in religious communities. It's a hunger we all carry, woven deep into the fabric of who we are.

Almost immediately, I was taught who the acceptable preachers were, which music was deemed holy, how to dress, and which doctrines were to be embraced or discarded. The five points of Calvinism became my mental scaffolding. I memorized answers to questions about suffering, hell, and why women or LGBTQ+ folks were supposedly unfit for leadership.

There were cracks in the logic, places where my spirit felt unsettled, but I believed that if I wanted to belong—not just to this community but to an eternal one—I had to think and believe rightly. And right belief wasn't found in curiosity or questions; it was found in compliance. I accepted this because I was taught that the church wasn't like "the world." We were set apart and no longer vulnerable to its lusts and distractions. We were called to die to our "old selves," distancing ourselves from anyone who might tempt us to stray, who might lure us into sin.

Before I knew it, my loyalty to the church eclipsed my relationships with family and old friends, who I now saw as lost in their worldly ways. I pushed them aside to chase the high of worship and the security of belonging to this new community. I didn't see how fragile this belonging was though, how it depended not on love but on conformity. As Brené Brown reminds us, when belonging demands that we reject, abandon, or distance ourselves from certain people, it isn't about true connection at all but about control and power.[1]

The disillusionment came slowly. I started to see that the church wasn't so different from the world we claimed to be separate from. People lied, hurled insults in anger, and gossiped behind closed doors. Some cheated on their spouses. The only difference was that in the church these sins were disguised as concerns and prayer requests, cloaked in the language of love.

When I became a leader, I thought my voice would carry weight. But any opinion or question I had that didn't align with the hierarchy was met with suspicion. Even though I was trusted as a leader, the moment I spoke anything that challenged power, I was silenced. Outside the church, I encountered similar dynamics—patriarchy, machismo—but in the church the expectation that I should defer to male leaders wasn't just cultural; it was also spiritual. Hierarchy wasn't merely tolerated; it was ordained. And because I was a woman, staying in my place wasn't just expected, it was a price I paid to belong.

———

A few years into my time in white evangelicalism, as the disillusionment began to take root, I had a dream. Or maybe it wasn't a dream at all but a vision of sorts. A reckoning. I can't say for sure. All I know is that it has stayed with me, lingering in the corners of my mind.

In my dream, I wandered alone through a dark forest, vulnerable and exposed. The trees jutted out of the earth like daggers. I don't know what I was searching for, only that desperation clawed at me, urging me to find safety. Then, in the distance, I saw someone. Relief surged through me. My legs were shaky, but I ran toward them, aching to know I wasn't alone. As I drew closer, I could make out their form—arms, legs, a face. All I wanted was to feel their presence, to touch them, to know they were real. But as I approached, something felt wrong. They stood there, still, unmoved. No fear, no reaction. *Are they okay?* I wondered. *Am I?*

With my arms outstretched, I collided with the figure, but instead of the living warmth I longed for, I felt the cold shock of plastic. A mannequin. I pulled back, gasping for air, my heart racing. Desperately, I looked for someone else. But no matter where I turned, I found only more mannequins—empty, lifeless bodies. Soon, I was surrounded by them. I touched their faces, ran my fingers through their synthetic hair, and broke down in anguish.

When I told my friend Katie about the dream, her blue-green eyes widened. "Whoa," she whispered. "That's heavy." We were sitting in our usual spot, an old, worn-out community room in the women's dorm. Red carpet, a musty smell, and aging furniture set the stage for some of our most vulnerable conversations. It was in that room I first dared to use the word I hadn't spoken aloud before: *cult*. We called it the C-word, something so scandalous we whispered it across the faded couch, knowing full well the weight of that admission.

That dream, though, I couldn't shake it. If I had to describe what it felt like to be a Latina woman in a white, conservative Southern Baptist seminary in the Deep South during Donald Trump's rise to power, it would be that vision. I was surrounded by bodies yet utterly alone. My subconscious was trying to tell me something: I was in the midst of people who appeared to offer belonging, but it was hollow. I was desperate for true connection. And I was beginning to realize the problem was not just an individual church or institution but the whole system. The weight of an empire in disguise was bearing down on everything, on all of us.

That world required a constant need to perform. Everyone was expected to keep up appearances because any sign of humanity would mean you weren't worthy. Sure, "grace" was preached to your face, but whispers of judgment always echoed down the hall. Trying to maintain the facade was crushing, and the shame that followed was disorienting.

Life within Christendom can often feel like a show, with the gospel itself treated as just another commodity for manipulation. It's all about sustaining the image we've created for ourselves and for God. As Pete Enns says, "For many, the failure to utter before God where we really are and what we really think reflects a lifetime of corrupt spiritual teaching: God went through a lot of effort to save you, so the least you can do is have your act together so as not to disappoint him. In a perverse twist, 'holding on to the Gospel' can become a motivation to hold on to self-deception."[2]

The dream woke me up to the realization that I was contorting myself into something I'm not in order to chase a hollow version of belonging. And I was doing so under the shadow of the modern evangelical empire—a culture that in many ways mirrors the way political empires at large have functioned: as a force so powerful it swallows many of us whole.

———

Evangelicalism isn't the only subculture that asks for perfection as the price of admission. In her book *Trick Mirror*, Jia Tolentino argues that the hyper-visible internet culture imposes similar pressures. Drawing on sociologist Erving Goffman, she explains that each person puts on a certain performance depending on who's watching. "The self is not a fixed, organic thing," writes Tolentino, "but a dramatic effect that emerges from a performance. This effect can be believed or disbelieved at will."[3] Offline, we find moments of relief in private spaces where we can let down our guard, costumes half removed and smudged makeup still on our faces. But online, we encounter a demand for performance, with no reprieve and an ever-growing audience. The performance isn't just for a potential boss or a best friend. We're performing for childhood frenemies, antagonistic family members, our kid's teacher, *all at once.* These dynamics feed the rise of trolling, cancel culture, and hate speech. There's little space to make mistakes, to learn, or to extend grace to those who do. The fear of being "found out" lingers like a shadow that refuses to fade.

What makes this even more unsettling is that we're being surveilled, tracked, and sold. Corporations that collect and sell our data send us curated content that feeds us what it thinks we want and tries to convince us we need more. This system looks for our insecurities and exploits them. Like evangelicalism and political empires, it thrives on the fear of not being, liking, or thinking the right things. The fear of not belonging.

Because we live in a world run by capitalism, these systems also prevail because they're profitable. Evangelicals have built a sprawling market around their culture: movies, conferences, T-shirts, even home decor. Evangelical consumer culture is inseparable from capitalism. In this way, empire—whether modern evangelical or American—has permeated everything, sustained by carefully crafted images and facades. It's all part of the same performance, with lights, cameras, and fog machines keeping the illusion alive.

The Modern Evangelical Empire

Speaking from a business management perspective, marketing consultant Peter Drucker has said that megachurches are "the most important social phenomenon in American society in 30 years."[4] Their strategies echo the executive offices of for-profit businesses, shaped by the same hiearchies that govern them. Megachurches, then, become a significant case study of how power, among other things, operates within an imperial framework.

Some trace the roots of the megachurch back to sixteenth-century Protestantism, but the modern American megachurch rose to prominence in the 1980s. It offered congregants a one-stop destination for spiritual, emotional, educational, and even recreational needs. What sets megachurches apart isn't just their size but their use of marketing-driven models to expand their reach.[5]

While today's megachurches and the Roman Empire of the first century are worlds apart, their shared impulses are hard to ignore. Both are built on the relentless pursuit of growth, the drive to expand into new territories, to draw more bodies into their fold. In this logic, numbers are proof of favor and evidence of being blessed. But expansion requires buy-in, which is why spectacle becomes essential. Rome understood this well. Processions, games, and theatrical productions were central to cultural life. Likewise, megachurches orchestrate their own grand displays—lights, fog, worship that feels more like a concert—to draw people into the experience. But the true strength of the megachurch, like empire, isn't in the spectacle itself. It's in those who give themselves to it, the devoted subjects who make its reach possible.

Another parallel emerges in the making of messiahs. In ancient Rome, the emperor reigned with unchecked authority, casting himself as protector and guide. He bore the *euangelion*—the gospel—a title later reclaimed in subversion when Jesus was named the true bearer of "good news." Emperors wished to occupy the space meant for God alone, even to the point of proclaiming themselves demigods. The echo of this in our political landscape today is undeniable. We anoint leaders as saviors, entrusting them with our security, our prosperity, our moral order.

The Hebrew people, too, fell into this longing, pleading with Samuel for a king like the nations around them, hoping a ruler would give them protection and peace. But Samuel issued a warning: A king would take their sons for war and their daughters for service. He would tax their fields, seize their vineyards, and claim their labor. He would make them servants in their own land (see 1 Sam. 8:11–17). Samuel tells them what history has borne out time and again, people suffer under the hands of those who wield power over them. Yet the people still insisted that they wanted a king to fight their battles.

This is how we learn power. It is generational, embedded in the ways we are taught to measure safety, success, and worth. A king offers security in the weight of his sword, the reach of his land, the force of his law. He gives the illusion of order and protection even as he builds his own name with the bodies of his people. Empire has always promised salvation through power. It is the nature of kings to offer belonging and purpose in exchange for obedience. It is the nature of a people to believe them.

In modern megachurches, pastors embody this kind of unchecked power, positioned as proxies for God—often without true accountability. They become untouchable, larger-than-life figures, wielding immense platforms and acting as the sole arbiters of doctrine and theology. And, like kings, we place our trust in them.

But pastors are more than just spiritual leaders, they are also entertainers. As Katelyn Beaty notes in *Celebrities for Jesus*, once a pastor's image is projected onto screens across multiple campuses, the pastor is no longer merely a teacher of the Bible; they are expected to captivate and sell ideas, experiences, and even products.[6] In this, they risk becoming icons of authority rather than shepherds. Like kings and emperors before them, they stand in for God, and the people—hungry for certainty—too often mistake their image for the divine.

No matter where you stand on the political or theological spectrum, it's hard to ignore the power of modern evangelical churches. After the rise and fall of figures like Mark Driscoll, Carl Lentz, and countless others, many of us find ourselves asking, "How did we get here?" How did a small, ragtag group of people, once figuring out how to organize themselves as a new community, evolve into a world power that shapes US culture, a modern-day empire? How did Jesus, a humble teacher who was killed by the empire, become a symbol of victory and military might, deeply tied to colonialism and some of history's most horrific human rights abuses?

There's much we can't be certain of, but one thing is undeniable: Christianity holds immense influence today. Churches dot our landscapes. "In God we trust" is stamped onto our currency, and the phrase "under God"—inserted into the Pledge of Allegiance in 1954—serves as a constant reminder of how deeply religious language is embedded into our civic identity.

The 2024 Paris Olympics ignited controversy when many Christians interpreted a scene in the opening ceremony as a mockery of the Last Supper. Featuring drag queens and dancers gathered around a long table, the performance sparked outrage, prompting Olympic organizers to issue an apology, even though the scene had nothing to do with Jesus. It was, in fact, a depiction of Dionysus, the Greek god of wine and revelry. The ceremony's artistic director described it as intentionally "subversive," meant to underscore "the absurdity of violence between human beings."[7] Yet, the backlash and subsequent apology revealed the immense power

Christians—particularly in the United States and the broader Western world—continue to wield.

So I ask again, "How did we get here?" The answer, as you might suspect, lies in empire. Christianity was born under it, in the time of Caesar. Though Christianity was a persecuted movement under Nero, it gained strength and legitimacy when Constantine made it the official religion of Rome. Many scholars argue that Constantine strategically adopted Christianity to serve his political agenda, recognizing it as the most advantageous religion to align with the imperial cult.

As we'll explore throughout this book, much of the Bible—especially the New Testament—shows us what it means to follow Jesus and seek true belonging under the shadow of empire. No, not all the letters and stories offer us clear-cut, anti-imperial manifestos. Instead, they are complex and ambivalent texts written by and for a people struggling to make sense of who they are within a system of hierarchy, domination, and greed. Much like today, empire in the ancient world was so pervasive that the early church couldn't envision a world without it.

Skilled at the Facade

In 2023, a viral social media trend had people asking how often men think about the Roman Empire. The answer was "quite often."

Historian David Perry suggests that our modern fascination is driven not only by the wealth of books, podcasts, TV shows, movies, and video games on the topic but also by the way people over the centuries have invoked Rome's mythic legacy. That legacy has been used to justify everything from slavery to the foundational principles of the US Constitution, like the separation of powers and the establishment of the Senate. The architectural influence of Rome endures in the fluted columns of neoclassical US government buildings and antebellum plantation homes. Perry notes that some people are deeply invested in an imagined Roman past, one that supports a white supremacist narrative. Donna Zuckerberg, author of *Not All Dead White Men*, argues that this fascination stems from the belief that Rome was the origin of "Western Civilization," a concept used to celebrate the cultural dominance of white men.[8]

Of course, other empires existed before Rome, but most were fragile and short-lived. Alongside China and Egypt, Rome established lasting bureaucracies, legal systems, and cultural expansion that impacted everyday life in a more established and enduring way. The Roman Empire's influence persisted long after its collapse, particularly through its institutions and religious impact. The very system that sustained its power, its reliance on exploitation and wealth extracted from conquered peoples, is ultimately what led to its downfall.

Rome's rise was relentless. It expanded through a series of hard-fought campaigns, becoming a warrior state by the second century BCE. Each new victory brought vast riches seized from defeated enemies. These gains, along with the revenue accumulated from taxation, were used not only to fund more conquests but also to proclaim Rome's growing power.

Rome's need for validation was central to empire building. The city became a monument to its own glory, filled with statues, temples, and arches that celebrated victories and the spoils of war. It was the quintessential narcissist, constantly exaggerating its achievements and talents in order to validate its existence. If you've ever visited Rome, you've seen its self-admiration: Striking monuments and structures proclaim its supremacy at every turn.

One of the highest honors in Roman politics was the triumphal procession, which consisted of a lavish parade through the capital to celebrate victorious generals. These spectacles were designed to glorify Roman power. Conquests were reenacted for cheering crowds and issued stark reminders of the defeat that awaited those who defied Rome. Scholars have suggested that this is the context behind Jesus's triumphal entry into Jerusalem on Palm Sunday, days before his crucifixion. In a subversive twist, it is Jesus who is hailed as victor and savior, riding into the city on a humble donkey—an act in defiance of Roman authority.

Years later, the Roman Empire held a grand procession to mark an event that would reshape both Jewish and Christian history: the destruction of the Jerusalem temple in 70 CE. For the Jewish people, the loss of their religious and political center led to a redefinition of Jewish culture to ensure its survival. For Christians, this event set the church on a distinct path, separate from Judaism.

After sacking Herod's temple, Emperor Vespasian and his son Titus desecrated the holy by parading the sacred vessels, including the Torah, through the streets of Rome. This celebration of triumph and exaltation over a vanquished people was immortalized at the Forum, the center of day-to-day life in Rome. Titus's brutal suppression of the Jewish revolt earned him an arch, a lasting symbol of imperial dominance.[9]

Rome's processions, along with its porticos, libraries, temples, statues, baths, theaters, and inscriptions, were meant to impress onlookers with the glory of Rome. What's worse, the battle scenes depicted on various monuments reinforced Rome's self-image as a civilizing force, masking the violence of its expansion by emphasizing the benefits of war. This is part of the image that empire constructs about itself; it is not an agent of violent conquest but a savior of the world, blurring the lines between aggressor and defender. In the telling and retelling of its own expansion, Rome was rarely the antagonist. Instead, their wars were fought as sensible and reasonable matters of homeland security. Rome justified the horror it inflicted on millions by calling it self-defense.[10] This strategy echoes still today.

American culture has glorified conquest, downplaying the brutality of the European invasion of North America. Consider the way schoolchildren wear feathered headdresses and black-and-white paper hats on Thanksgiving, reenacting the Pilgrims and Native Americans coming together for a peaceful feast at Plymouth.

This narrative is not only filled with inaccuracies, it is also far from harmless. This depiction erases the atrocities of colonialism, particularly the five hundred years of violence against Native Americans and First Nations peoples. The Wampanoag Indians, whose society was deeply damaged by the Pilgrims' arrival, are especially affected by this mythological retelling. Each year, Natives gather at Plymouth Rock, not to celebrate Thanksgiving but to observe a National Day of Mourning.

The celebration and glorification of conquest runs deep in Roman identity, with roots in the founding myth of Romulus. Centuries later, Julius Caesar carried this tradition to new heights. In 46 BCE, he staged one of the most extravagant triumphal processions in Rome's history, a twelve-day spectacle of lavish festivities honoring his far-reaching military campaigns. The slogan of this triumph—*veni, vidi, vici* ("I came, I saw, I conquered")—is still one of the most famous Latin phrases today.

Language matters. If we pay attention to the phrases, idioms, and metaphors we use daily, we see how deeply the violence of empire permeates our thinking. Consider these common expressions: We "pull the trigger" when making a final decision and "bite the bullet" when doing something unpleasant but necessary. We're "killing it" when we succeed, and when we make a mistake, we've "shot ourselves in the foot." If we fail badly, we've "bombed." We "launch" ideas, "target" audiences, and "deploy" resources, using the language of weaponry and warfare even in creativity.

This language is far from neutral. The ethos of conquest is embedded in the way we talk, think, and even worship. For many Christians today, a victorious Savior who plunders his enemies, even through violence, is welcomed and celebrated. Just think about some of the most common worship songs sung in many churches today. Most are replete with language about triumph, conquering, battles, and victory, drawn from images in the Bible, especially in the book of Revelation.

The Roman Empire's dominance extended into every facet of life in the ancient Mediterranean world. Religion, politics, economics, and social structures were inseparable, creating an all-encompassing system that shaped daily life for early Christians. As a result, every page of the Bible was written under the shadow of empire.[11]

Scripture is full of imperial imagery and ideology, even when it's subverting it. The imperial metaphors—including submission, warfare, and rulers—have shaped Christian identity and practice for centuries, sometimes in ways that tether faith to power. These words have been wielded to justify colonial expansion, racial exploitation, and systems of exclusion, framing even God in the image of an emperor or religious ruler.[12] It's a paradox: A text meant to equip communities to resist empire has also been used to uphold it.

To confront this truth is not to discard the sacred but to reclaim it, to unravel the imperial threads woven into our faith and Christian identity and ask what remains. This is the first step toward liberation, toward a vision of God and community unbound by dominion. Only when we acknowledge empire's hold on us can we imagine a kingdom where power no longer conquers but heals.

An Imperial Imagination

The book of Revelation shows how deeply empire is etched into the imagination of the biblical authors. Even in its most radical denunciations, John's text uses the very language and ideology of the empire it seeks to critique. For Christians, Revelation is the promise of a final victory over evil, the climactic moment when those in Christ will *reign* with him in the new Jerusalem, treading streets paved with gold. This anticipated *triumph* shapes much of Christian hope, woven into worship songs, sermons, and whispered prayers for redemption. And so, perhaps, this is the best place to begin: at the very end.

Revelation is often read as a fearless critique of the Roman Empire, one that proclaims its ultimate downfall. When John names Rome "Babylon," he's not just identifying an empire; he's mocking it, stripping it of its grandeur and exposing its monstrosity. Babylon—Rome's caricature—is not only a city but also a beast, its power rooted in satanic forces. This parody has a name: *catachresis*, which means the deliberate misuse or misapplication of language.[13] It's how the oppressed borrow the symbols and language of their oppressor, twisting and mocking them to reclaim power.

We see this even now. In Latine culture, the word *chingona* was once a slur used to demean assertive women, while its masculine form, *chingón*, was a compliment. But *chingona* has been reclaimed, transformed into a badge of honor for women who defy patriarchal expectations.[14] *Catachresis* takes the tools of empire—its words, its symbols—and creatively repurposes them to resist.[15]

Revelation brims with such subversions, even in the use of the word *empire* (*basileia*) itself. But the parody doesn't stop there; the simple declaration "Jesus is Lord" is political dynamite, defying the emperor's claim to divinity. The greeting "worthy are you" (see Rev. 4:11), once reserved for Caesar, is now sung to God. And the twenty-four elders casting their crowns before the throne (4:10) is an echo of Emperor Domitian's bodyguards bowing in submission. These acts unmask the pretensions of imperial power, showing its fragility when faced with divine sovereignty.

But here's the tension: John doesn't fully escape the logic of empire. At first glance, Revelation seems less like the destruction of empire and more like a mere exchange of rulers—Caesar's reign for that of the King of kings, a divine kingdom in place of a human one.[16]

John's vision of the new Jerusalem as the ultimate paradise, a place many Christians hope for as the end of evil and injustice, begins to resemble the empire it claims to replace. In Revelation 22:15, the gates of this city are closed to those deemed immoral. Only the righteous belong, while the unrighteous are left outside.

This exclusionary dynamic feels uncomfortably familiar, more like an empire redrawn than one dismantled. Look closer and the vision of heaven shimmers like empire itself: gates of pearl, streets of gold, foundations of precious stones. An emperor's dream. Is this liberation or a sanctified empire?

Audre Lorde's phrasing comes to mind: Can the master's tools dismantle the master's house? If the new Jerusalem still depends on creating insiders and outsiders, then what has truly changed?[17] Empires have always been built on hierarchies. Rome placed its elite at the center, calling the rest barbaric. The British Empire did the same. The United States, too, has its margins, where those deemed "other" are left to struggle for a semblance of dignity.

Even John's climax—celestial battles marked by war and violence—raises questions. Can violence truly undo violence? Can a kingdom built on exclusion and bloodshed ever be called just? Or is it simply a mirror of what came before? Can we replace one dualistic empire with another and call it freedom?

This paradox challenges us to reflect not just on the structures of past empires but on the spaces we attempt to create in response. Are they truly liberating, or do they quietly replicate the same dynamics of exclusion and hierarchy we claim to resist? It's a call to ask uncomfortable questions, to wrestle with the ways power operates within us and around us: Do we re-create patterns of domination in our leadership, where decisions are top-down rather than collaborative? Do we unintentionally center the voices of those already privileged? Do we treat resources—money, time, attention—as something to guard, hoard, or compete over rather than share generously? Do we re-create patterns of burnout, perfectionism, and overwork in our institutions or even in our family culture? Do we police belonging, perpetuating dualism and an us-versus-them mentality?

These are the questions we must wrestle with, especially when the imagery of empire has so deeply shaped us, as it did in John's world. If our faith rests on the promise of a new kingdom that casts some people out, it's no wonder that, throughout history, Christians have followed suit—drawing the same borders, keeping the same hierarchies intact.

Lynn St. Clair Darden, a Black postcolonial scholar, sees this pattern even in many justice movements. Liberation scholars, with their hearts tuned to the cries of the oppressed, often speak of a God who stands fully on the side of the downtrodden. But Darden offers a warning: This way of thinking often reinforces the same binary structures inherent in empire. The oppressed are exalted, the oppressors disgraced. The hierarchy shifts, but it remains unbroken.[18]

In our zeal to dismantle power, we risk reconstructing it, locked in cycles that push some to the margins. So how do we read Scripture or seek justice without being seduced by empire's logic? Darden calls us to a different kind of liberation, one that lives not in the clean lines of binaries but in the tangled tension of human life.[19] Justice isn't a reversal of roles; it's a disruption of the whole system.

This is why resisting empire begins in imagination. It's daring to dream of a reality entirely brand new: disrupted, shaken, free.

A Sanitized Incarnation

Empire's greatest strength is the illusion that it alone can save us, bring us peace, and offer us belonging, as long as we pledge allegiance to its ways. This illusion thrives in our politics and in our theology. Christianity itself has been edited and sanitized, its antiseptic images infiltrating our view of God and ourselves. Take the incarnation, for example, the bedrock of our belief system.

I gave birth to my first child just before Christmas in 2021, and after the whirlwind of childbirth and those early days of motherhood, I found myself unable to fully engage with the Advent season. The words I'd grown up with—hope, joy, peace, love—felt so distant. I felt them with my child, of course, but I was also exhausted and overwhelmed. In a culture that offers little support to new mothers, it was hard to find rest or reflection. Advent came, and I struggled to make sense of it.

But then it struck me: Advent is more than the shallow embrace of peace, hope, joy, or love. It's not just about the easy parts of anticipation; it's also about the waiting, the wrestling, the tension. It's about living in that holy discomfort and grappling with the uncertainty of what comes next.

We're taught that Advent is about the anticipation of Christ taking on flesh. Shouldn't it then be a season in which we're the most connected to the tenderest parts of our humanity? Especially if we're struggling? The truth is that Advent's ideals are hard to hold on to in a world that's sold us their cheaper versions.

Empire is all about appearances. It hands us a shallow story of hope, leaving people hopeless. It claims a false peace, built on destruction. It frames love by conditions such as "hate the sin, love the sinner," a phrase that often conveys more harm than grace. What we're given is a love that keeps people in their place, which isn't really love at all. And joy? It's sold to us as a future ideal, something we experience in a life yet to come.

No wonder we struggle to feel these things in a world that devours us. We live suspended between what is and what could be. But maybe that very tension—that ache, that wrestling—is exactly where the divine meets us. Perhaps the hope and love we long for, the kind that transcends understanding and defies empire, is found in refusing the hollow versions we've been handed. We wait for something new to take shape in us: in our bodies, in the world. Just as Mary did during that first Advent, bearing the weight of the divine within her.

The image we're given of Christ's birth is pristine—a serene manger, a baby wrapped in soft cloth, animals standing in quiet reverence. And while it might be sweet, it's far from true. This isn't just a harmless Christmas scene; it's an illusion, a smoothed out version of the story shaped and molded by empire.

Because the Bible is a book written by men, it shouldn't surprise us that the story of Christ's birth is told in ways that overlook the reality of childbirth. It focuses on angels and shepherds but skips over the blood, the pain, and the fear. We miss the primal groans, the strength it takes to bring life into the world. That matters because the full humanity of the event is stripped away. The incarnation—God becoming human—is about divinity entering the brokenness of the world, in the midst of life's fiercest realities.[20]

We talk about Jesus's body being broken for us while sometimes forgetting that Mary's body was broken for him. Divinity entered the world through a Brown, female, refugee body—a body that was vulnerable, stretched, marginalized. And that's where divinity still shows up today, not in sterile or sanitized scenes but in the untamed places of our lives.

Our faith is rooted in the human, the holy, and the hard. The nativity story as it has been presented to us misses the grief, the sorrow, and the longing that are just as much a part of this world as joy and love. Life, like birth, is both painful and beautiful, sacred and profane.

So yes, it matters how we tell this story. It matters because it shapes how we see the sacred. We've been taught that holiness is uncontaminated by the dirt and pain of real life. But is that how divinity truly enters the world? No, it enters in the mess and rawness of our humanity.

If you visit Bethlehem today, this truth is even more poignant. The modern city is now encircled by an eight- to nine-meter-high separation wall, with only one entrance and exit, transforming it into both a ghetto and a city prison.[21] In the West Bank, separation walls wind around cities and slice through Palestinian farmland, keeping Israeli settlers apart from the Palestinian population.

The street artist Banksy once called Bethlehem the "least Christmassy place on earth."[22] In 2017, the year marking one hundred years since the British took control of Palestine, Banksy opened the Walled Off Hotel on Caritas Street, near Manger Square, where

Christ is traditionally believed to have been born. Until the horror erupted in 2023, this site stood as a fully functioning hotel, museum, and art gallery—just steps away from the illegal Israeli West Bank wall. The hotel itself was a subversive piece of artistic protest, also used to put money back into local Palestinian projects.

The same year he opened the hotel, Banksy teamed up with director Danny Boyle to create an "alternativity," a powerful critique of the sanitized scene we're used to—and of the illusions empire feeds us. In the film, local Palestinian children wear Santa hats and angel wings and sing "Jingle Bells" under fake snow. Joseph receives a text message from the angel, and a glowing Mary rides a donkey onto the stage. All of this unfolds with the imposing gray barrier of the separation wall behind them. As the play ends, a woman remarks, "Jesus was born here in Bethlehem to bring peace to mankind. Well, let's say . . . he's still working on that."[23] Some parents laugh, brushing off the fake snow, while others wipe away tears.

The birth of Jesus, like our lives, was fleshly and carnal and offensive, and it was also holy. It's in *this* space where we find and experience the divine, where the divine became human and dwelled among us. And what does that say about God? Empire—both American and Christian—has mastered the art of selling us a facade. It feeds us hollow representations of who God is, what faith, life, and spirituality should look like. But when we take a close look at the birth of Jesus stripped of the filters, we're confronted with a truth that calls us to reject these false narratives.

The holy angst we carry is not something to ignore but a sacred stirring. It must be named, lifted like a cry in the wilderness, so that we might unearth what is real and step into the kind of freedom and belonging that empire could never offer.

———

I look back at that night at the evangelical conference with complicated wonder. Was it real? Or was it manufactured, an illusion crafted by the lights, the guitar solos? Whatever it was, it undeniably changed me. Since then, my theology has evolved, and the way I worship has shifted, but I can't dismiss the power of that night. Some call it a "thin space"—a place where heaven and earth collide, where the lines between the physical and the spiritual blur, and time and space feel suspended. These thin spaces become markers in our lives, moments we carry with us forever.

I was reminded of this once at a book signing, when a woman approached me seeking advice on how to talk to her children about their heritage. "I'm a proud Mexican American," she said, "but I choose to be here." Her voice softened with a trace of defeat. "How do I talk to my kids about this? I want them to be proud of where they come from, but there's a tension when we talk about what drove us to leave and the realities that keep us from going back." I spoke to her about empire, about the systems of greed that exploit and terrorize, that force people to make unimaginable decisions for their survival. But what I most wanted her to understand was this: Those systems don't have the power to define the richness of our cultures, our people, or the everyday experiences that make us whole. They don't get to have the last say.

That conversation has stayed with me, echoing the memory of my own "salvation experience"—that defining moment that shaped everything that came after. And here's the profound mystery of spirituality: It defies the barriers we build, especially those crafted by forces that seek to suppress. The Christian empire, in its hunger for God, gold, and glory, has wrought untold damage in the name of Jesus. Yet, in that mysterious, paradoxical way that only spirituality can accomplish, it has also broken us open beyond words. On that Friday night, in that building, I encountered something transcendent—something that still eludes my ability to fully describe. And it happened right in the midst of empire.

These are the moments that we must refuse to let empire, with all its tricks and gimmicks, take from us. They are ours. They belong to us both individually and collectively.

For years, as I deconstructed the colonial Christ, I spoke of that night with skepticism, maybe even a little shame, as if I had been tricked or lost myself in the moment. But now, I choose to claim it. I won't let empire's manipulations silence my truth. That night, I met Transcendence. I met Love. I encountered the Divine in a way I never had before.

That doesn't mean I hadn't met God elsewhere—at the altar of St. Dominick's Church with Abuela or praying the rosary on the floor at Yami's house. God was there too. But for reasons I can't quite explain, God also chose to meet me surrounded by thousands of people, amid fog machines, lasers, and a jumbotron. God works with us where we are. I believe now, as I write these words, that this was a necessary part of my journey. You can't deconstruct something—you can't truly critique it—if you haven't lived it, if you haven't breathed it and felt it in all its complexity. I needed to immerse myself in all its glory to then be able to turn it on its head, to be able to see past the illusion.

Prayer of Resistance

God of Unmasking,

We resist empire's illusions that offer a sterile holiness, a conditional love. Forgive us for the times we believed this, for bowing to false gods, for letting empire name us. Let your mercy fall like rain, softening the soil of our hearts. Allow us to receive forgiveness as renewal so that we might sow a new kingdom of justice, truth, and love.

For the times we have failed to see reality for what it is, open our eyes, O God.

Benediction

May fear release its grip and pride be surrendered so our eyes may be opened to see the world as it is and as it yearns to be. Ignite our imaginations with holy curiosity, for truth is a gentle flame, ready to burn away the facades. We commit to doing the work of exposing empire, trusting that in our honest reckoning we will find a path toward healing and wholeness.

Amen.

CHAPTER 3

Rejecting Ideology, Embracing Wisdom

Invocation

Sacred Wisdom, voice that hums through the fabric of the universe, ever ancient, ever true. We honor your quieted song, the silencing you've known, and we remember the power you hold, unbroken, waiting to be heard again.

We open our hearts, eager to receive the sacred gifts she whispers, the fullness of her embrace waiting to transform us.

Reflection

The Mi'kmaq people tell a story about the Great-Grandmother and her wisdom:

Nukumi, the wise and ancient grandmother of the Mi'kmaq people, lived alone in the forest. She was as old as the mountains and as knowledgeable as the rivers, but over time her strength began to fade and the cold crept into her bones. One day a large wolf appeared before her. Instead of fear,

45

*Nukumi felt a deep kinship with the creature, recognizing it
as a gift from the Creator. The wolf offered itself to her, and
with great reverence Nukumi accepted. She used the wolf's
fur for warmth, its bones for tools, and its meat to nourish
her weakened body.*

*As she prepared the wolf's remains, sparks flew from her
tools, igniting the first fire. The flames danced, giving her
warmth, light, and vitality. Nukumi understood that the
wolf had brought more than just physical sustenance. It had
gifted her with fire, a source of life and community. She carried this gift to her people, teaching them the sacredness of
balance, reciprocity, and respect for all living things. From
that day, fire became central to their survival and spirit.*

Those who have ears let them hear.

I left the megachurch I attended in Miami when its leaders
pledged to save twenty thousand souls by the year 2020. They
plastered that number everywhere—on the screens during worship, in the sermon notes, on their website. It wasn't subtle. The mission was clear, and how they resolved we'd achieve this goal involved
handing out invitation cards to anyone we came in contact with. I
often saw these cards scattered across tables at the nearby Starbucks.

One afternoon, I sat across from a church leader at that Starbucks, chatting about my involvement in small groups. The hum
of the coffee shop filled the air as we spoke, with the clink of mugs
and the quiet murmur of conversations weaving around us. My
companion paused mid-sentence, her gaze drifting over to a man
sitting alone at the next table. "I feel God telling me to give him
an invite card," she said with resolve.

She rose with urgency and handed the man the card, inviting
him to service on Sunday. The man politely accepted the card but

declined the invitation, mentioning he attended the synagogue down the street. When she returned to the table she leaned in, whispering with certainty, "I bet that invite is burning a hole in his hand. That's a seed planted." She took a sip of her drink, as if this was the most natural thing in the world.

I froze, caught between disbelief and embarrassment. It wasn't just the words that were spoken but the ease with which the man's faith was dismissed. This is how certainty and assumption can masquerade as love. It also became more clear than ever that this is what the church had become: a mission to get as many bodies as possible in the pews. We were to "save" people in the simplest, most quantifiable way possible, like faith was a metric to track more than a life to cultivate.

I left the megachurch that year, though in my heart I had left long before. I thought seminary would be the antidote. I hoped that being in the company of the "learned," around those who devoted themselves to "serious" study of the Bible, would cure my disillusionment. But in the world of academia, I found I had left one kind of empire for another. It turned out that the academy, with its mostly white male gatekeepers and intellectual elitism, was where the imperial roots of the church truly thrived.

Postcolonial thinker Homi Bhabha, reflecting on leaving India to study literature in the West, once said, "I went to Oxford to embellish the antique charms of the armoire; I ended up realizing how much I desired street food. Why was I intellectually fascinated but unmoved, when I found myself at the academic acme of the literary culture I had chosen to follow?" This is how I felt after a couple semesters in seminary, with the halls of red brick, the prestige, the formality. It all started to feel like a cage. Bhabha continues, "What one expects to find at the center of life or literature . . . may only be the dream of the deprived or the illusion of the powerless."[1]

Stepping into the world of scholars and theologians with their "robust" and "legitimate" faith, I, as a Latina woman from a family who spoke broken English, discovered that I'd bought into the illusion. The problem was that it didn't deliver what I had hoped. What I thought I needed was the very thing pulling me farther away from the divine. Instead, I found myself drawn to the wisdom of the overlooked, to the interpretations of those who had been ignored or pushed aside. They pointed me to Christ.

This realization is what led me toward the slow, steady, and ongoing work of decolonization.

What Decolonizing Isn't

In 2022, *Merriam-Webster*'s word of the year was *gaslight*. What was once a term heard primarily in therapy sessions had now entered the mainstream, largely thanks to social media.[2] This isn't necessarily a bad thing. Access to the basic tools of therapy via TikTok, Instagram reels, and podcasts has never been easier, and for that I'm grateful. Discussions about things like boundaries, abuse, and trauma are now less stigmatized, thanks to their frequent appearance in everyday conversations. But as these terms have gained popularity, experts have raised concerns about the rise of "therapy speak" and the casual overuse of psychological terms. When we overuse these terms, we risk misusing them and diluting their meaning and power.

When large groups of people think they understand a word's meaning, they tend to use it quickly and without care. This doesn't just water down the word; it derails important conversations that require nuance. Mental health professionals have cautioned against the rise of therapy language detached from its context, warning that it can become a kind of performance—an attempt to elevate one's experience by invoking the authority of psychological jargon. In doing so, we lose the nuance these discussions demand. When complex realities are flattened into labels, we risk creating barriers. Labeling others can stop us from engaging with them on a human level. Over time, this leads to isolation and fragmentation, which harm individuals and communities alike.[3]

This is how we end up putting people into a mental box and then throwing away the key. We cut off our belonging to one another when we reduce humans to objects by weaponizing terminology that was meant to liberate, to expand, and to heal. And isn't that the goal? Liberation for all of us as a whole.

The year 2020 catalyzed many social movements, most notably Black Lives Matter. It urged the global community to confront the systemic racism plaguing society in the wake of multiple videos documenting the killing of unarmed Black people. While People of Color have long declared "enough is enough," social media's reach combined with that year's stay-at-home orders reenergized the movement. Diversity, equity, and inclusion initiatives spread across industries, pushing the public to reckon with the colonial past of nations that were founded on the murder and subjugation of Black and Indigenous communities. Calls to diversify our bookshelves, workplaces, classrooms, and personal lives became widespread—and rightly so. Terms like *white supremacy* and *antiracism* entered the mainstream. While these concepts were not new to many, their broad use in public discourse marked a shift.

At the time, I was finishing a dual master of divinity and master of arts in theology, with a focus on postcolonial theology. Much of my coursework engaged postcolonial and decolonial thinkers who were disentangling academia from colonial ideology. I read works by thinkers from the global periphery, exploring how they might interpret biblical texts that are often discussed by those at the center. I wrestled with how my Western-influenced thinking shaped my understanding of the Bible, written from a non-Western perspective. How did living under the legacy of empire and colonialism influence how I saw faith and, more important, divinity? These same questions were bubbling up in the public sphere. While I was excited by the energy surrounding this call to action, I also shared the frustration of public thinkers who warned about the dangers of oversimplifying a term like *decolonize*.

It didn't take long for many to recognize that *decolonize* was being used in the same vein as *diversify*, oftentimes interchangeably. I once came across a popular social media platform challenging followers to "decolonize their bookshelves" by offering a list of books written by authors of color. While reading books from a diversity of perspectives is important and valuable work, it doesn't necessarily mean that we, or the authors themselves, are actively decolonizing and intentionally divesting from the ways of empire.

The danger of becoming viral is that terms like *decolonization* lose their depth and nuance. Decolonizing inherently includes hearing from a diversity of people, but the two are not synonymous. Decolonization is rooted in centuries of lived experiences, teachings, and perspectives that go beyond building a more diverse bookshelf.

The Journey of Unlearning

I recall the first time the question of what it means to decolonize began to take root inside me. At the time, I didn't have the language to name it a journey of decolonizing. I only knew that something deep inside me was stirring, connecting dots that had once felt so far apart. And with that stirring came a kind of pain that arises when the past begins to unearth itself, when history climbs up out of the grave, brushing off its bones.

In *Abuelita Faith*, I write, "Colonizer or colonized, oppressor or oppressed—there's a moment after the deep, dark, often lonely work of becoming our own archaeologists that the pangs hit. It's a surprising pain that often comes when we dig up the skeletons from the ground, when we realize the dirt we stand on is tainted and the reality we've been fed is curated."[4] I consider it a grace—and somewhat paradoxical—that this journey began for me while in seminary, right in the belly of empire. But as the saying goes, "God works in mysterious ways."

I imagine that, since you're reading this, you're already somewhere on the path of decolonization, whether just beginning or having journeyed for as long as you can remember. Wherever you find yourself, I hope you know that decolonizing is a lifelong process. For everything I continue to learn, there is just as much I'm working to unlearn.

Because we've never known a world outside the grip of colonialism, patriarchy, and capitalism, we're going to spend our entire lives holding the tension between them and the world we hope for. This is part of what I mean when I use the term *decolonize*: disconnecting from the status quo, from a theology that has been molded by empire, from a colonial Christ. And this journey isn't about "arriving" somewhere or "conquering" some ideal, for these very goals are remnants of colonial thinking, aren't they?

There's no simple formula for unlearning the ideologies that have seeped into our bones. It's an ongoing process of breaking free from a worldview that has shaped how we see God, ourselves, and others. That might feel overwhelming, but there's also something sacred in it. To live fully as a human is to always be in motion—always evolving, growing, learning. It's about allowing new perspectives to emerge and finding God not in the arrival but in the unfolding. In every step and stumble. In the becoming.

Decolonization, then, is not a destination but a constant movement. Accepting this frees us from the pressure to fix or solve and instead invites us into the holy work of unmaking the mindset we seek to dismantle. And that is its own kind of liberation.

In the words of T. M. Nahanee, a Squamish facilitator and strategist, "Decolonizing is like healing, it is different for everybody every day, there is no final endpoint, and it's not easy."[5] When I first came to this realization in my own healing journey, it felt like a release, freeing me to be more fully present in the process, to experience the grace of being in motion. This is where I experience the depth of my humanity—in the becoming. It is in this continual process that I dig deeper into myself and into the divine.

We live in a culture obsessed with destinations. We're so focused on where we think we need to be that we often miss the very moments that make the journey what it is, that shape who we are.

In this spirit, Nahanee, writing from an Indigenous perspective, offers four guiding concepts for decolonial work:

1. *Decolonizing* means unraveling the narratives we've inherited, challenging the beliefs and ways of knowing shaped by colonial forces. It involves asking hard questions about what we've been taught and why, and rejecting ideas that were imposed on rather than born from our communities. It might look like questioning the glorification of certain historical figures in schools or rejecting a faith practice used to silence people.

2. *Indigenizing* goes beyond a token nod to Indigenous wisdom; it is about fully centering it, letting it become a guide for how we live and how we love the land. It's about learning to care for the earth as kin. Maybe it's planting native seeds in the soil where we live, asking how we can honor and learn from its original stewards. To indigenize is to remember our responsibility to future generations, to live today as better ancestors.

3. *Reconciling* is about healing wounds, historical and personal, through acts of repair. It calls for Indigenous and non-Indigenous people alike to face the harms done, not just through apologies but through tangible actions. Maybe it looks like supporting land restitution movements or having uncomfortable conversations about the impact of colonialism in our communities. True reconciliation means facing the truth, no matter how heavy, and finding a path forward that restores dignity.

4. *Self-actualizing* is the journey of reclaiming ourselves—our names, our stories, our ancestors—as we strive to live in

fullness. It means stepping into who we were created to be, not as fragmented parts but as whole beings. It could be as simple as learning the meaning behind our family name or as profound as creating art that honors our heritage. It's about becoming, not in a way that's individualistic but in a way that ties us to those who came before and those who will come after.[6]

Potawatomi author Kaitlin Curtice reminds us that decolonization is both macro and micro: "We work to change the systems around us by first paying attention to our own surroundings."[7] Yes, it involves actions like voting, petitioning, protesting, and boycotting. But it also means attending to everyday details like picking up trash in our neighborhoods, recycling, buying from local artisans or farmers, paying attention to where our money goes, sharing meals with neighbors, and treating our bodies with care. These small acts are part of how we live into "on earth as it is in heaven," how we begin to repair what has been broken. To decolonize is to integrate mind, body, and spirit.

As you can see, decolonization is a deeply personal process with many pathways to explore, the term itself carrying a wide range of definitions and approaches.

Many Indigenous leaders argue that true decolonization demands the restoration of land to Indigenous peoples. The Land Back Movement speaks to this. It calls for returning ancestral territories to their original stewards, restoring their deep bond with the land, and empowering sovereignty. But it's more than land; it's reparations—a reclamation of power, wealth, and life for a people long displaced.[8] When we speak of decolonizing in relation to Native and First Nations peoples, this must stay at the forefront. It's the macro, the big-picture reality. Decolonization loses its meaning if we detach it from this vast, unwavering truth.

Empire hasn't just taken from us, in the way of land, cultural practices, and spiritual beliefs. It has also given us a lingering, toxic legacy of intergenerational trauma rooted in the exploitation of people and the environment.

To be colonized is to internalize empire's mindset and worldview. To decolonize, then, begins by divesting not only from colonial ways of being but also of *knowing*. Academia, where Western thought has been passed down, taught, and protected, has been a primary vessel for empire's ideologies. To truly decolonize, we must learn to hold space for Indigenous, Native, and non-Western *wisdom*—alternative ways of knowing that are just as valid. As the National Inquiry into Missing and Murdered Indigenous Women and Girls affirms, decolonization means resisting colonial forces and recentering Indigenous values and philosophies.[9] It's about undoing, yes, but also reimagining, finding our way back to the fullness of who we've always been.

Making Room for Other Ways of Knowing

The Bible speaks urgently and abundantly of wisdom. Proverbs tells us to find it (3:13), hold fast to it, and love it, because wisdom will care for us and keep us safe (4:5–6). Wisdom is not some distant, stoic thing; she is imagined as a nurturing figure. Wisdom is a woman crying out in the street, in the public square, at the entrance of the city gates, calling to any who will listen (1:20–21). This is no quiet plea but rather a summons. A reckoning. This powerful image is why I believe it's important for us to pay attention, to remain curious, to dare to listen to what wisdom wants us to hear.

But before we can do that, we must be able to answer the question, *What is wisdom?* And perhaps more urgent, *Who gets to define it?*

Western culture has long crowned itself the gatekeeper of knowledge, deciding what counts as truth and whose voices are worthy of being heard. This is about epistemology—how we know what we know. Theologian Willie James Jennings observes that the Western ideal of the "educated" person has long been a white, self-sufficient man whose worth is measured by his power to possess, control, and master.[10] Even the title "master's degree" carries the weight of this ideology. In theology, the name implies that we somehow can—or should—seek to master the divine. The absurdity of this hits me every time my credentials are shared, as though they validate my worth or my nearness to God. In fact, if there's anything I do know after years of studying divinity in the academy, it's that the words *I don't know* are a sacred declaration.

Western theological education, steeped in white dominance, has traditionally clung to the idea that other voices are not only inconvenient but somehow less holy. The logic of empire believes it it has a duty not just to teach but to *save*—to civilize what it deems barbaric. This same thinking has elevated the West as the pinnacle of wisdom, driving technological innovation while suppressing other forms of knowledge and the communities they're born from. But true wisdom cannot flourish in a system that values mastery over mutuality, control over connection, or power over the kind of understanding that is born from lived experience.

———

In the thick forests of South America, the people knew something that the colonizers failed to see: The bark of the cinchona tree was a healer in disguise, holding within it the power to cure fever, to fight the unseen terror of malaria. For generations, the Native people had harvested this gift from the earth, crushed the bark, and mixed it into tonics that kept the sickness at bay. The practice displayed an intimacy with the earth, an embodied knowledge passed down in whispers from one generation to the next.

But when the colonizers came, they sought to measure the worth of a people by the extent to which they could be controlled. They looked at this people and called them backward, primitive. After all, what could the "uncivilized" know about healing?

Yet when the fevers blazed through European communities, no amount of Western faith or science could stop the burning. Relief came from the bark of the cinchona tree, medicine that had long been known and used by the Native peoples. And so, gratefully, they took it. But soon, that gratitude gave way to control. They began to peel back the layers of the tree, seeking to extract this Indigenous knowledge and turn it into something profitable. Quinine, they called it. A sacred remedy, now stripped from its roots.

Decolonizing knowledge is about remembering the wholeness of the things we have dismembered. It's about acknowledging that the same people whose wisdom saved countless lives were also the ones whose stories and spirits were deemed dispensable by the very hands that benefited from them. In the rush to extract and exploit, colonizers missed the deeper truth: Restoration is not just about the cure but about connection—to the land, to each other, to the histories that hold us.

So when we speak of quinine today, we remember that this medicine is a testament to the power of Indigenous knowledge, a reminder that the earth has always whispered healing to those willing to listen. We do others a disservice when we dab the bark on our wounds but refuse to honor the people who first gathered it. Healing is in the remembering.

———

Western knowledge flows from assumptions we often carry without question, beliefs so engrained that they become our worldview, sometimes without our even realizing it. In the West, for example, knowledge is disciplined and rigidly compartmentalized. It is rooted in "objective truth" and the desire to chart every detail of reality like a map on a flat surface. It also sees the world in binaries: setting good against evil, separating the human soul from the body, and distancing nature from spirit. Western knowledge is linear, time running in a single direction with each tick representing some sort of "progress."[11] These habits of thinking have crept into how many Western Christians read the Scriptures and walk their faith. The Bible easily becomes another text to be mastered, measured, turned into a formula rather than a living Word. And in this way, some have taken on a faith that seeks to conquer rather than transform, to dominate rather than dwell.

But the Bible itself reveals a truth often overlooked: Divine wisdom is not confined to one culture or people. Many of the sayings in the Bible's wisdom literature echo the insights of neighboring ancient societies. Take Proverbs 22:17–24:22, which parallels the *Instruction of Amenemope*, an Egyptian wisdom text dating back to at least the twelfth century BCE that offers guidance on how to live with humility, integrity, and care for the vulnerable. The Hebrew authors did not reject these principles but instead wove them into their sacred texts.

In doing so, they remind us that wisdom transcends boundaries, that truth can be found in unexpected places, even beyond our own traditions. This is a quiet decentering of exclusivity, a recognition that knowledge belongs to no single people. Instead, it is a gift to be shared and honored across cultures. Perhaps this is the heart of wisdom itself: an openness to learning from the "other," without fear, in a sacred exchange that resists the grasping hand of empire.

In many non-Western traditions, knowledge is as fluid as it is sacred. Here, knowing is not a concept but a way of moving and being in a world that insists wisdom lives as much in the soil and the wind as it does in human thoughts. It is intuitive, born of intimacy between land and people. It understands the rhythms of daily life—wisdom held by Indigenous, rural, urban, and often female voices. In these traditions, knowing resists becoming a purely intellectual exercise, insisting instead that wisdom is embodied, as natural as breathing. The mind is never seperate from the body; here, wisdom is felt before it is spoken.[12]

Take South Africa, where the memory of apartheid looms large. In this place, traditional healers, *sangomas*, hold a kind of knowledge long dismissed by the West. During apartheid, when South Africa's government enforced segregation and oppressed non-white South Africans, these healers were labeled primitive, their medicines and rituals pushed aside to make way for the sanitized methods of the West. But after apartheid, a sacred pulse began to beat again. The South African government began to recognize the *sangomas* and their deep well of wisdom, honoring their role in the communities and lives of so many.

Healing, for the *sangomas*, reaches beyond herbs and potions. It lives in drumming that recalls ancient rhythms, in dances that summon a kind of presence that defies containment, in rituals that call forth ancestors as a form of memory, of healing. For them, wisdom cannot be sterilized or sealed away in textbooks. It is alive, breathed in song and spoken in heartbeat, passed from body to body, recalling something older than words.

This is not a knowledge we can dissect in a lab. It is a knowing that lives in the bones, echoing through the flesh. It's the wisdom of a people who know that to remember is to be transformed. As the Asaro tribe of Indonesia and Papua New Guinea say: "Knowledge is only a rumor until it lives in the muscle."[13]

Scripture affirms this. The Hebrew word *chokhmah*, often translated as "wisdom," isn't mere intellect. It's the artisan's skill, knowledge that shapes and reshapes us just like a potter's hands reshape clay. It is intuitive, bodily, born from lived experience and survival. And *yada*, another Hebrew word that means "to know," doesn't speak to facts or analysis. It's the knowing between lovers, the ache of closeness. This knowledge is felt and sensed, with an intimacy far deeper than data.

This can feel unsettling to the Western mind because it challenges the idea that truth is a fixed, unchanging thing. But in many non-Western traditions, truth is dynamic and alive. It is rooted, yes, but it evolves and unfolds over time. Truth is something we discover more deeply as we move through life. I watch this reality unfold in my young daughter day by day as she comes into her own understanding of herself and the world. Her truth develops with each new encounter, each quiet revelation. It is a becoming—a slow attunement, deepening as we grow, mature, and learn to listen to the wisdom unfolding within us.

This embodied knowing is a call for the oppressed to voice their reality in their own language, without translation or dilution. It's a truth-telling that transcends divisions between Western science and Indigenous wisdom: two currents that, if allowed, can thrive together, honoring the distinct ways each understands life and creation. Only when these wisdoms move in harmony can we hope to build a world in the image of those who have been silenced, a world transformed by voices that carry truth from bone to breath.

Where Knowledge Becomes a Weapon

We come to understand the world through the stories we tell. In many cultures, this has long taken the form of oral tradition, wisdom passed from mouth to ear, generation to generation. In Western contexts, where oral traditions often carry less weight, the written word holds powerful sway. The books we champion or ban shape how we understand life, belonging, and history. Whose stories are told? Whose are silenced? Decolonization begins here, in the radical act of valuing the stories of the oppressed, not as charity but as a reclaiming of the fullness of human wisdom.

In recent years, book banning has surged in the United States, with nearly ten thousand instances of book bans within just a two-year span, according to groups like PEN America and the American Library Association.[14] Censorship's hand falls heaviest on authors from marginalized communities, narrowing their presence in the very spaces where they are most needed. The books most often targeted are those daring to speak on race, gender, and sexuality. The works of Toni Morrison, Maya Angelou—stories of Black identity, resilience, and truth—are deemed "explicit," unsettling the comfort of a dominant narrative that prefers silence to the messy beauty of honest storytelling.

Book banning is about more than specific books; it's part of a broader struggle over who has the right to define truth in education, who can speak into our cultural consciousness. Censorship reveals an ancient anxiety that certain ideas or perspectives might threaten power structures. Throughout history, there has always been a tension between controlling information and safeguarding freedom of expression. One of the earliest recorded acts of censorship traces back to authorities under Roman rule burning Protagoras's works in the fifth century BCE because they spoke of his agnostic views. And in the early Christian era, non-Christian texts were suppressed under Constantine's reign, with the First Council of Nicaea condemning writings that contradicted Christian orthodoxy. Entire histories were erased, silenced, and denied a place in the canon of memory.

From ancient Rome to modern America, the battle over who gets to tell the story—whose voices are honored and whose perspectives are feared—reveals a tension far deeper than mere words on a page. It's a struggle over what we believe is worth knowing, worth remembering, worth living by.

———

Books have never been just books. In the hands of empire, literature didn't merely entertain or inform. Through stories, empires controlled social narratives, solidifying their power to define and shape the way civilizations understood themselves.

At the heart of it all was language itself. English, sharpened into a weapon of control, was one of empire's most effective tools. As Bill Ashcroft notes, the rise of English as a prestigious academic subject wasn't accidental, it grew in step with the British Empire's expansion in the nineteenth century. Studying English exposed individuals not only to a language but also to an entire worldview—a subtle propaganda that painted Western knowledge as truth. It created a world where language communicated as well as indoctrinated.[15]

As literature produced what was considered "objective knowledge," colonial narratives wove the tale that conquest was not only necessary but also beneficial.[16] This is Eurocentrism: the insistence that European ways of thinking are the world's anchor. And with that comes the belief that non-European languages, cultures, and traditions are not only inferior and less valuable but also that the people who practice them are less rational and intelligent.[17] Even though Western culture is just one culture among many, others are measured according to Western standards and ultimately judged as falling short.[18]

Stories about European heroes that portray native people as in need of "civilizing" were told in order to justify the occupation of foreign lands. But they weren't merely stories, they were revered as cultural canon. Consider Alexander the Great carrying *The Iliad* with him on his conquests, drawing inspiration from its battles and characters as if it were a holy script.[19] Novels like *Robinson Crusoe* and *The Jungle Book* glorify European explorers and conquerors as divinely favored, while native populations are portrayed as not only carnal but also voiceless. Women became symbols representing lands and people who yearned to be claimed and possessed by the colonizer, as in the tale of Pocahontas and John Smith—a story of conquest through romance.[20]

And so, if literature helped plant the seeds of empire, then freedom's work must also start in the realm of stories. It's not enough to dismantle empires; we must also confront and unlearn the toxic ideas these stories spread. Writers, readers, and educators are called to challenge the stereotypes, myths, and Eurocentric fantasies that have long defined colonized people in these texts.[21] Because in the end stories are about power, and we hold the choice of which ones will shape our future.

What About the Bible?

As we explored earlier, the Bible has long been entangled with empire's ambitions. Some even suggest that its very structure—the way it was gathered, ordered, and bound—bears the imprint of imperial influence. A "canon" is never neutral. It creates boundaries, deciding which stories and voices are lifted and which are left in the margins. In its design, a canon reflects the authority of those who compile it.[22] The Bible we hold today did not fall from the heavens intact; it was assembled by those in power, with certain texts deliberately included while others faded into obscurity.

Yet, despite this, the Bible itself isn't inherently a tool of colonization or decolonization. It holds within it a tension where conflicting voices born from political, social, and spiritual struggle collide.[23] The New Testament emerged from a church in conversation—and often in conflict—with the Roman state. Those who assembled it were shaping not just theology but identity, seeking to define themselves under imperial rule.[24]

After Constantine made Christianity the official religion of the state, the church was no longer just a marginalized movement; it became part of the machinery of power. Soon, Christian symbols fused with imperial imagery and leaders enjoyed its privileges, framing the cross as a symbol not of sacrifice but of victory. The idea of a Christian emperor, who ruled under divine sanction, became central to the church's rhetoric. Through councils, creeds, and excommunication, the church used the mechanisms of empire to exclude other forms of knowledge and assert control over "truth."[25] The New Testament was used to perpetuate this hierarchical framework. Once a collection of writings for a persecuted people, it soon became essential for consolidating power within the church hierarchy and solidifying orthodoxy. It became a tool for empire to define who belonged and who did not.[26]

In this process, some voices—especially those of women—were pushed aside. Consider Mary Magdalene, whose leadership among the disciples is preserved in the Gospel of Mary, a text deliberately excluded from the canon. In silencing her, the church didn't just alter its sacred texts; it reshaped the role of women in Christianity itself.[27]

───────

Even though the Bible was compiled by people under Babylonian, Assyrian, Persian, Greek, and Roman rule, many biblical scholars still haven't reckoned with how imperialism informs how we read and interpret these texts.[28]

Scripture, like all literature, holds multitudes. Some of its stories carry the weight of imperial ideologies, while others pulse with the promise of liberation. To read it with open hands, rather than clutched fists, is to understand that no single interpretation can exhaust its depths. This allows it to become not just a rule book but a rhythm, alive and unbound.

Decolonizing the Bible isn't about replacing one interpretation with another or simply inverting the power dynamics we've inherited. It's about holding space for a mosaic of perspectives to coexist in tension, resisting the urge to tidy them into resolution. It's a refusal to demand that Scripture make us comfortable or certain.

Consider the contrast beween Ezra-Nehemiah and Ruth. In Ezra 9–10, the prophet laments that Israel has intermarried with foreign women, describing it as a form of impurity that threatens their identity. In response, the leaders command these marriages be dissolved, sending away foreign wives and children. This text reflects a deep anxiety about survival under imperial rule, where maintaining a distinct identity was seen as necessary for preserving the people of Israel.

Then there's Ruth, a Moabite who is one of the very people Ezra sought to exclude. But instead of being cast out, Ruth is drawn into the story of God's people. Her loyalty, her labor, and her love secure her place in the lineage of David. When we read Matthew's genealogy of Jesus, Ruth is honored by name.

These passages resist resolution. One clings to separation as faithfulness; the other stretches the story of God to make room for the outsider. To decolonize the Bible is to refuse to smooth over these tensions, to sit with the reality that Scripture is not a single voice but a chorus—full of contradictions, complexity, and truth. Wisdom is not always found in simplicity or certainty but rather in the willingness to listen, especially when what we hear unsettles us. It is an invitation to free both the text and ourselves from the binaries that keep us bound.

And what's profound is that Ruth herself carries a wisdom that unsettles. Her very presence defies the boundaries drawn to dictate belonging. In the persistence of her love and the boldness of her survival, she reveals that wisdom is often forged in the margins, in the lives of those the world overlooks. Ruth doesn't fit into the neat narratives we might wish for; instead, she inhabits the tension that is found when the expected and the excluded collide, showing us that wisdom is found in the courage to move within the in-between.

It is in these tensions and this nuance where the richness of wisdom emerges, not by erasing contradictions but by dwelling in them, by allowing new knowledge and understanding to take root.

Life Flourishes on the Edges

I remember once, sitting on the edge of the shore, watching a crab move slowly along the beach. It was fascinating to see how it navigated the terrain: the shifting sands, the crash of waves, and the sharp edges of the rocks. It seemed to have mastered the art of adaptation—living in that space between water and land, between two worlds. I thought about how the crab didn't try to dominate either space but instead thrived by embracing the tension between them.

In many ways, this is how we must begin to decolonize knowledge, by searching for wisdom not from the center but from the margins. Just like the crab living between worlds, knowledge at the edges offers something profound. It's in those spaces where the dominant narratives are challenged and where the boundaries blur.

Ecotones are geographical places where two ecosystems converge in a kind of sacred overlap. They are edge zones, where a forest and a meadow brush up against each other, where the ocean embraces the shore. Ecotones are defined by constant cycles of deconstruction and reconstruction. They are spaces of resilience, teeming with the richness of creation that arises from the friction of different worlds colliding. It's curious, isn't it? In these places of tension—where one world constantly gives way to another—life flourishes in abundance.

Life on the edge is more adaptive because it has to be. Species that learn to survive in environments that are ever-changing become the most creative. This is why ecotones are called "zones of opportunity," places where life thrives not in spite of the tension but because of it. Conservationists recognize that by protecting these liminal spaces, they safeguard the broader web of life.[29]

Ecotones whisper to me of resistance, of refusing the forces that seek to confine and control. Western ways of learning have long convinced us that knowledge is universal, that it flows from the center, from empire, as if wisdom must be dictated from above. But nature teaches us otherwise. Wisdom thrives at the margins, in the spaces between, where different ways of knowing collide and something altogether new begins to emerge. To decolonize knowledge is to turn our gaze toward the thresholds where survival and tension have given rise to a deeper understanding of the world. Here, wisdom waits, not in the polished certainty of empire but in the raw becoming of those who dwell at the edges.

Nature, our own experiences, and even Scripture confirm this truth: When we nurture these sacred in-between places—both spiritual and physical—we create opportunities for flourishing. It is at the margins, where the center cannot reach, that divine wisdom breathes most freely, transcending words and logic. It's a wisdom that pulses through our veins, that resides in our very marrow, reminding us that life thrives in the tension, in the ecotones of the soul.

Prayer of Resistance

God of Our Ancestors,

Forgive us for the ways we have misused or neglected the sacred knowledge of our ancestors. We want to unlearn the lies that bind us and weave a new tapestry of knowing. Let us move with tenderness in every step, rising in defiance and knowing that liberation begins in the reclamation of our minds.

We stand firm against the erasure of our truth, refusing to let it be silenced. With every breath, we honor the wisdom that shapes us.

Benediction

May we open our hearts to the knowledge that flows from the unlikeliest of places, from voices we never expected and hands we've never met. Let us surrender to the quiet gifts they offer, recognizing that wisdom often arrives in the most humble of forms, ready to teach us. We commit to learning from those who have been told they have nothing to teach us.

Amen.

CHAPTER 4

Rejecting Hierarchy, Embracing Kinship

Invocation

Voice in the Margins, we long to reject the hierarchies that divide us. Teach us to behold one another fully, not as greater or lesser, but as kin, woven together in love, and held in the sacred dignity of shared breath and becoming.

We are one family, created equal in the divine image.

Reflection

The tribes of Alta and Baja California tell a story of a mighty cougar and a tiny cricket:

> *Cougar was strutting through the forest when he leaped onto a fallen log to survey his kingdom.*
>
> *"Get off the roof of my home!" Cricket said as he emerged from the log. "You're crushing the roof, Cougar, and my lodge will collapse!"*

Cougar, irritated but curious, stepped off. He bent down toward the insect. "Who are you to tell me what to do? I am the chief of the animals."

"Chief or not," Cricket replied, unshaken, "I have a cousin who is mightier than you, and he would avenge me."

Cougar sneered. "I don't believe you."

"Believe me or not," said Cricket, "but it's true."

"Fine," Cougar challenged. "Bring your cousin tomorrow at noon, and we'll see who's stronger. If he fails, I'll crush you and your home."

The next day Cougar returned and waited impatiently by the log. "Where's your cousin?" he demanded. Just then, a tiny mosquito flew up from the log and buzzed into the big cat's ear. "What is this?" cried Cougar. The mosquito began to bite Cougar's inner ear and drink his blood. "Ahrr! Ahrr!" cried Cougar. "Get out of my ear!" Cougar pawed at his ear and ran around in circles shaking his head. The mosquito bit him again and again.

Cricket called up, "Will you leave my lodge alone now?" Defeated, Cougar agreed and ran off.

Those who have ears let them hear.

Systems sustain themselves through hierarchy. I saw this unfold on an ordinary Tuesday morning at our local community center, where I had settled in to work on this very manuscript. Most of the members and staff are People of Color, while the leadership is predominantly white. As I typed, I witnessed a young Middle Eastern man who spoke little English being berated by his white supervisor. It wasn't just a correction; it was a public humiliation, and it left me disturbed to my core.

I was compelled to speak up, so I found a manager I felt I could trust, a Black man, and through tears explained what I had just witnessed. "I'm sorry. I just had a baby, and I think my hormones are all over the place," I added. The tears were real, but the apology was reflexive. I wasn't sure why I felt the need to apologize for feeling so deeply. He assured me I had nothing to be sorry for, but I felt vulnerable. I told him, "My family comes here because it feels like a safe space for People of Color, but what I saw today didn't make me feel safe—as a woman or as a Latina." I was still crying.

"I hear you, ma'am," he said. He promised to address the situation, and I believed he would.

But as I returned to my laptop, I still felt unsettled. I realized how deeply hierarchy had shaped that entire encounter. It was evident in the way the young man was treated, in the power his supervisor wielded over him, and in my own impulse to apologize to a man for my emotions. Even in a space that is supposed to feel safe, the architecture of hierarchy is built into every exchange. Hierarchy is not just about power over someone else; it's about how we internalize that power—how we learn to shrink ourselves, to apologize for being human, and how we carry the weight of it even when we try to resist.

———

Not all hierarchy is unnatural. Some forms emerge from the rhythms of existence itself, perhaps even as a means of survival. Consider Maslow's hierarchy of needs, the pyramid that illustrates the way our bodies first seek food, water, and safety before reaching for love, belonging, and self-actualization. It's a morally neutral way of ordering human flourishing. There are countless other examples like this in the fields of biology, architecture, and design. Even in the natural world, hierarchies are undeniable; I could tell you exactly which one of my chickens rules the roost and which is at the bottom of the pecking order. Some hierarchies are simply the way things are.

But when hierarchy becomes a tool to exploit, dominate, and degrade, it distorts something natural into something unnatural. Power is wielded to control resources, and those in power often act to acquire more.[1] This desire becomes insatiable: The more power they have, the more they crave, and the more they're willing to harm others to keep it. The vulnerable bear the mental, physical, and emotional cost of this greed.

The church is no stranger to abusing hierarchy in search of power. From as early as the second and third centuries on, church hierarchies have informed the daily life of Christian communities. Those with less—whether the poor, the enslaved, women, or children—have been exploited. The Protestant Reformation arose, in part, as a reaction to this, with Martin Luther opposing the selling of indulgences, a practice that preyed on the most vulnerable by offering eternal assurance for a price.

Even today, Protestants claim the "priesthood of all believers," but hierarchy is woven into the fabric of many American churches. I'll never forget being scolded by a pastor at a Southern Baptist church for getting together with young women to read the Bible without asking his permission. It was clear then how gender hierarchy functioned as a mechanism of control.

Within both Catholic and evangelical traditions, church is often seen as an extension of the family, with pastors and leaders positioned as spiritual "fathers" who must be obeyed. The danger lies in how these structures of authority are wielded to silence and subjugate.

American Family Hierarchy?

There is a strange grace in the absurdities of parenthood, one that comes in unexpected forms—like memes scrolling across a screen. On days when the weight of parenting presses down hard, these little moments of humor remind me that we are never as alone as we feel. One meme, in particular, haunts me. It says, "Me and my partner thinking back to when we thought having kids was going to be soccer games and matching outfits, not unpacking our trauma." The image shows two people doubled over in hysterics, faces cupped in disbelief. And it's true—some of the most profound liberation work I've ever done has been through parenting.

This is the work of decolonizing, isn't it? Peeling back the layers of empire's reach into the most intimate parts of our lives and souls. So much of what we carry comes to light when we enter the realm of parenting, where the wounds of generations become visible. Research affirms what many of us already know deep in our bones: Trauma is passed down through child-rearing.[2] There's a history to this, a deep wound rooted in the belief that from the moment of conception, children bear the weight of sin. Some traditions speak of babies as born into guilt, carrying Adam's shame in their tiny bodies. You'll hear some say, "No one has to teach a baby to sin," as if the cries for love and attention, the declarations of "Mine!" are proof of corruption.

I, too, used to be convinced that the selfishness of children was evidence of a deeper evil. "Look at the way they demand! It's all me, me, me," I would argue. But there's more to this story, and it has nothing to do with the burden of sin and everything to do with the reality of growing and becoming.

To be sure, parenting a toddler isn't for the faint of heart. But that's because toddlers are learning. Their tiny minds are absorbing the world at a rapid pace, picking up language, understanding their bodies, discovering new emotions. It's a sacred process that requires tenderness and patience. What some might call selfishness is really just the emergence of autonomy. These small humans are discovering who they are—separate from us. And in that discovery, they're learning to trust, to explore, and to belong.

Yet for those entrenched in theologies that prioritize control, this time of discovery can be seen as something to crush. The goal is not to guide them but to break them. Toddlers aren't nurtured; they are subdued. This is the belief behind books like *To Train Up a Child*, which became popular in many evangelical circles in the late '90s and early 2000s, during a time when so-called "biblical parenting" was gaining traction. It emphasized strict discipline, obedience, and parental authority as divine mandates. Families like the Duggars, who gained fame on their reality TV show, practiced these methods: placing toys just out of a baby's reach, smacking them when they grasped for it. Or they would pull their infant's hair if they bit, even accidently, while nursing.[3] These responses are rooted in the belief of a child's inherent rebellion; they're designed to strip away autonomy, to conquer the will of the child before it can take root.[4]

The Duggars and some other Christian parenting "experts" point to Proverbs 22:6, "Train up a child in the way he should go: and when he is old, he will not depart from it" (KJV), to explain their approach. But for many, this training looks more like the breaking of animals than the nurturing of a soul. Corporal punishment becomes a tool of control, and though it may bring about obedience, research shows it rarely brings about the deeper moral integrity we long for. Instead, it results in weaker internalizations of morals and values and poorer parent-child relationships.[5] In the end, parents who use these methods achieve the opposite of what they intend, even when they use the Bible to justify their actions. More troubling are studies showing that corporal punishment leads to higher levels of aggression in children, teaching them that conflict resolution involves imposing one's will on another—an association that persists into adulthood.

This pattern of control seeps into our churches. It is no wonder that many pastors replicate what they learned as children: the use of fear and intimidation to maintain order. The well-behaved child becomes a representation of the well-behaved church—a place where the nuclear family is upheld not only as the bedrock of society but as a deeply political symbol.

But parenting, like faith, is about trust, discovery, and liberation. And perhaps when we loosen our grip, when we make space for our children to be fully human, we find that we, too, are being liberated.

———

Many evangelicals believe they're called to preserve the strength of American families. As Billy Graham famously stated, "A nation is only as strong as her homes."[6] This conviction fueled the political resurgence of "family values" starting in the 1970s—a powerful convergence of fears and anxieties about race, gender, sexuality, and power. By the close of that decade, patriarchal authority, steeped in a cultural wariness, had become a defining feature of evangelicalism. Christian media became the vehicle for teaching parents how to raise their children and whom or what they should fear along the way.[7]

For many evangelicals, a well-ordered home was the foundation of both morality and security, and the "correct" family was patriarchal.[8] In this evangelical worldview, Satan was out to destroy the American home, a significant threat because the home is the training ground where children learn to submit to authorities and governing structures. Children were raised to know their place in a divinely sanctioned hierarchy. In essence, family values were all about the reassertion of patriarchal authority.

The turbulence of the 1960s signaled to many social conservatives, including many evangelicals, a generation of youth rebelling, not just against their country's unjust laws but against the authority of the family itself.[9] Influential figures like James Dobson, John MacArthur, and Bill Gothard began warning parents that the future of the nation depended on how well parents, particularly fathers, could control their children.

This was unfolding as more women were entering the workforce and divorce rates were rising. But rather than addressing the obvious economic forces at play, evangelicals zeroed in on gender roles and authority as the core of this crisis.[10] It wasn't economic restructuring that worried them; it was the loosening grip of patriarchal control.

Gothard promoted a divinely ordained "chain of command" that mirrored military hierarchies. He taught that the church, too, should mirror this structure, with leaders wielding unchallenged authority over their congregations.[11] In essence, he drew a straight line from the home to the pulpit in enforcing obedience.

Gothard often used visual metaphors, such as his umbrella diagram: Christ above all, followed by the father, then the wife, and finally the children huddled beneath. Rain, depicted as the attacks of Satan, falls from the edges of the umbrellas—an odd choice considering rain is viewed as a blessing in the Bible. But the message was clear: Authority flows from the top, and only through submission can one remain protected. Many evangelicals believe Gothard's assertion that hierarchy is divinely ordained. But when I look at the way Jesus spoke to his followers, I see something different.

In the Gospel of Luke, the disciples are squabbling over who among them should be considered the greatest. Jesus's response is striking in its simplicity. He points not to the structures of power they are familiar with but to something entirely different: "The greatest among you must become like a person of lower status and the leader like a servant" (22:26). Jesus directly challenges their notions of power. Greatness, he says, is not about lording authority over others. It is about humility, about lowering oneself to serve.

Perhaps then, authority looks less like Gothard's umbrella and more like a root system in which strength is drawn from below. The roots, buried and unseen, are what sustain and nourish life above. Without them, the tree withers. True power is found not in dominance from the top but in the humility of grounding oneself, of lifting others up, of drawing life from those often overlooked.

In the Gospel of Matthew, Jesus goes further. When asked who is the greatest in the kingdom of heaven, he points not to kings or priests but to a child. "If you don't turn your lives around and become like this little child," he says, "you will definitely not enter the kingdom of heaven. Those who humble themselves like this little child will be the greatest" (18:3–4). Jesus doesn't reinforce the hierarchies of his day; he subverts them, placing the vulnerable and the small at the very center of the kingdom.

This is the kind of authority Jesus modeled, one rooted in tenderness, connection, and service. It's a vision that many evangelical leaders have missed in their pursuit of power, mistaking submission to human authority for faithfulness to God. True authority, Jesus seems to say, is about becoming like a child—humble, open, grounded, and deeply attuned to the source from which all life grows.

Not Your Father's Hierarchy

It's hard to talk about family structures in the West without feeling the pull of ancient Rome, where its shadows still linger. In Rome, discipline and strictness were seen as virtues, tools to forge adults who could endure hardship. The Roman family, built on a foundation of hierarchical authority and rigid obedience, planted seeds that would grow into the patriarchal systems still present in many Western models.

Roman imperial structures were influenced by Plato's idea of human hierarchy. The household was a mirror of society, and within it were distinct roles: father over children, husband over wife, master over slave. The household was so central to maintaining Roman peace that laws were created to protect it. These household codes weren't just social norms; they were legal systems reinforcing the hierarchy. When we encounter the household codes in the New Testament, we see a framework that's already deeply embedded in the culture. Those writing and receiving these letters were grappling with how followers of Jesus should engage with and respond to this cultural structure.

Take Ephesians 5, which says that wives must submit to their husbands. But just before that, it says that all believers, men and women, are to submit to one another out of reverence for Christ. Mutual submission was a radical shift from the Roman household codes that demanded strict hierarchy, with only one—the father—having ultimate authority. Ephesians 5 disrupts this by speaking to *every* member of the household. Instead of granting authority to one man who speaks and acts for his household, the Christian household codes grant each member agency and "the right to hear and act for themselves."[12]

Paul himself embodied this tension between tradition and transformation. He was a complicated figure, toggling between supporting empire and resisting it. He wasn't fully aligned with the imperial structures, but he also wasn't entirely outside them. His writings reveal both a longing for liberation and dutiful adherence to the constraints of his world. To engage Paul's work with honesty and care is to resist the urge to reduce him to either a revolutionary or a mere enforcer of empire, recognizing instead a man shaped by both revelation and limitation.

When it came to women, Paul was neither a feminist nor a staunch defender of patriarchy. He found himself caught in the tension between the two, a tension that becomes clear when we read his letters with care.

In 1 Corinthians 7:4, Paul writes that a husband's body belongs to his wife, a shocking statement for his time. In a world where a husband had nearly unchecked control over his wife's body, Paul is saying no, this power is shared. This reveals the egalitarian nature of the kingdom of God, where authority is redefined. And yet, in 1 Corinthians 11:5–10, it seems Paul is upholding gendered practices by instructing women to cover their heads while praying, grounding his reasoning in creation order.

Perhaps the most powerful challenge to the imperial order comes in Galatians 3:28, where Paul declares that in Christ there is no male or female, no slave or free—a radical vision that upends the social hierarchies of his time. If the household is a microcosm of the state, what kind of world might take shape if families lived as if this were true? It would be something unrecognizable to Rome, something that threatened the very foundations of its rule.[13]

The teachings of Ephesians 6 also subvert hierarchy in the relationship between parents and children. In the Roman world, the paterfamilias held absolute power over his household, including his wife, children, and any enslaved people under his roof. This authority mirrored that of the emperor over the people of Rome. Any threat to the father's authority was seen as a threat to the stability of the state.[14]

When children are instructed to obey their parents in Ephesians 6:1, it might seem like a reinforcement of the existing structure. But the focus shifts when fathers are addressed directly, "Don't provoke your children to anger" (6:4). In a society where a father's power was absolute, this call is one for restraint, urging fathers to avoid using their authority simply because they can. Mothers aren't left out either; the teachings suggest a kind of shared power within the family—a power-with, not a power-over.

Power-with is mutual. It requires listening, respecting, and honoring the dignity of each person, no matter their age or status. It means that if we want respect from our children, we must respect them in return. Power-with creates a culture of empathy and cooperation, not domination through fear or force.

Both in the Roman Empire and today, children have been among the most vulnerable and marginalized, bearing the weight of empire's obsession with control and hierarchy. Because they are at the mercy of those who hold power over them, children are frequently regarded as "less than," subject to abuse and exploitation. In many systems, they are seen as property or mere extensions of their parents.[15]

In my own childhood, the principal's office had a designated spanking chair and a wooden paddle. Children were subjected to corporal punishment for "misbehavior." Offenses deemed punishable were subject to the interpretation, whim, demands, and mood of the teacher, who could label any behavior bad on any given day. Imagine if those fixated on God-given authority took the Bible literally—as they encourage others to do—and refrained from provoking children to anger. What if they rejected an authority rooted in hierarchy, which both Jesus and Paul seem to subvert?

When Jesus speaks of greatness in the kingdom of God, he doesn't point to emperors or generals; he points to children. If our parenting and our relationships were built on that vision of power, then our households would more clearly reflect the kingdom of God instead of the ways of empire.

———

Piety—*pietas*—was one of the highest virtues in the Roman world. It was the cornerstone of how society understood duty, family, and citizenship. A child's obedience to their parents reflected this virtue. *Pietas* demanded a kind of reverence that wasn't merely respect but a giving over of oneself to the will of the parent, even when that will was unjust. In the Roman imagination, parental authority was near divine, and children, like women and the enslaved, were by nature meant to be ruled.

Fathers didn't just wield symbolic power; they owned everything. Children, no matter how old they were, held nothing in their own name as long as the father lived. A father could dissolve his children's marriages at will. The boundary between childhood and adulthood was blurred, particularly for daughters, who were expected to obey their parents for life. In many ways, these structures of hierarchy—rooted in patriarchy—remain with us today, shaping how family members relate to one another, particularly in cultures in which honor and respect for elders hold significant weight.

In my own community, the sentiment of the perpetual child persists. For example, many Cuban families function with the unspoken rule that adult children—especially women—are to submit just like their younger selves did. Respect and honor flow up the family hierarchy but rarely down. This was a struggle for me as I navigated my own life. So much of the weight of childhood expectations clung to me long after I'd outgrown them.

But here's the tension. While I deeply value the wisdom of our ancestors, and I write about this in *Abuelita Faith*—about the sacredness of our family stories, especially the ones marked by struggle and survival—I've also learned that part of being fully human involves reckoning with the wounds inflicted by patriarchy, colonialism, and the rigid hierarchies that have shaped our families. Healing from these systems doesn't dishonor our ancestors; it honors the fullness of our, and their, humanity. It acknowledges that while our elders may have survived great traumas, some of those traumas were passed down to us, unintentionally yet profoundly.

I once spoke to a group of students of color in Philadelphia about survival and the wisdom of our ancestors. A young man raised his hand and asked, "What if I'm the first one breaking generational curses and wounds in my family? What would you say to someone who's trying to heal from them?" The room grew quiet. His question held a holy weight. It shook me.

I told him what I have told my own inner child over the years; healing is a sacred act of courage. Honoring our elders doesn't mean we can't also name where they failed us. We can grieve the places where they upheld their own oppression or where the trauma of their survival became the weight we now carry. To live in a decolonized reality is to receive the wisdom and gifts of our ancestors with one hand while gently laying down, with the other, the harm they may have caused.

To that young man, I said what I've told myself over and over in the slow, painful work of healing from colonial and patriarchal wounds: "I'm so proud of you."

———

Few communities on Turtle Island carry the scars of colonization like Native populations, particularly the children who were torn from their families and cultures. The Doctrine of Discovery drove some of the most grievous abuses against Indigenous peoples. Issued by Popes Nicholas V and Alexander VI and becoming a global principle beginning in the fifteenth century, this doctrine asserted that Christians had both the divine and the legal right to invade and seize lands inhabited by non-Christians. It fueled the belief that Indigenous people were so uncivilized that their children would be better off if they were taken from their families and put in Christian schools.[16]

Throughout the nineteenth and twentieth centuries, governments across the United States, Canada, and Australia executed plans to "educate" and "Christianize" Indigenous children. They did so by forcibly removing them from their homes and sending them to residential boarding schools. These schools, hundreds of them, were created through partnerships between the governments and Christian organizations. Governments funded them, and Christian denominations provided the labor—teachers, priests, nuns. The stated goal was chillingly simple: "Kill the Indian, Save the Man."[17]

What happened in those schools was beyond sinister. Children were stripped of their names, their languages, their cultures. They were sexually and physically abused, starved, tortured. Many didn't make it out alive.[18] The discovery of unmarked graves, like the two hundred found at a former residential school in Canada in 2021, is a haunting reminder that the trauma is far from over. These abuses have left a legacy of intergenerational pain, fracturing Native communities and entrenching social and economic disadvantages that persist to this day.

Christianity played a significant role in this initiative, just as it did in the genocidal campaigns against and enslavement of African and Latin American peoples around the globe. This systemic violence is part of the broader evil of colonialism, and the church was not merely complicit but central, a pillar that held up the entire colonial system.[19]

I think of Nelson Mandela's words here: "There can be no keener revelation of a society's soul than the way in which it treats its children."[20] How we care for children—how we honor their dignity and humanity—"is and always will be a fundamental measure of a society's strength, well-being, and wholeness," of its very soul.[21] And in this history, we must reckon with the ways the church failed to protect the most vulnerable. This reckoning, however painful, is necessary if we are to seek any meaningful healing or reconciliation.

Racial Systems of Hierarchy

The suffering of Native children in residential schools lays bare how oppression intertwines and how hierarchies embed themselves into cultures. In early Christianity, the treatment of the enslaved and the treatment of children were closely linked, shaped by marriage laws and imperial control.[22] Hierarchies don't stand alone; they create a vast, oppressive web that keeps us all bound up within it.

Plato's *Republic*, written in 360 BCE, laid the groundwork for Western beliefs about human hierarchy, which later influenced concepts of race and racial categories. For example, Plato introduced the idea of the "noble lie"—a myth designed to uphold the social order as divinely ordained by claiming that people are born with different metals mixed into their souls (gold, silver, iron, or brass) that determine their place in society. While Plato's focus was primarily on class hierarchy, it set the stage for later ideas about inherent differences between human beings, which would evolve into racial categories.

Thinkers of the Enlightenment era drew on Platonic ideas to classify new racial hierarchies based on skin color. Not long after, in the United States, the Three-Fifths Compromise in the Constitution reduced enslaved Black people to a fraction of a human being, while full citizenship, the right to vote, and agency were reserved for white men.[23] What began as a philosophy of class in ancient Greece had evolved into a system that upheld racial oppression, enshrined in the laws and beliefs of the land.

What makes racism so insidious is that it's so deeply embedded in the story of the West that it can feel impossible to imagine life

81

without it. But it hasn't always been this way. There was a time, in the early years of European colonization of the Americas, when the racial caste system as we know it didn't exist. The concept of race wasn't a given; it was something that had to be constructed. It took deliberate effort by those in power—politicians, church leaders, intellectuals—to create the idea that skin color could determine one's humanity, their freedom. Over time these ideas took root. Europeans, including Christians, codified these beliefs into laws and social habits that concentrated power in the hands of those they deemed "white" while denying equality to those they labeled "Black."[24] Christianity played a tragic role in this construction, often associating skin color with sin or unbelief and twisting Scripture to justify oppression and exclusion.[25]

—————

Rachel Held Evans once observed, "The New Testament household codes tend to get sliced and diced. . . . Rarely are they read, or discussed, in their entirety."[26] We often do this with texts that make us uncomfortable, whether passages about women, children, or, perhaps most disturbingly, slavery. The debates that raged in the nineteenth century among pastors and congregants over the Bible's stance on slavery sound eerily familiar to the ones we hear today. Abolitionists were accused of not taking the Bible seriously enough when they advocated against slavery. Besides Ephesians 6, Philemon was often cited as evidence that the Bible supported it.

Philemon is a brief letter nestled within the New Testament, but it has a complicated and contentious history. On the surface, the letter seems straightforward: Paul, writing from prison, urges Philemon, a fellow believer, to welcome Onesimus, a man returning to him after some unexplained dispute. Philemon, who owes some moral debt to Paul, is being asked to receive Onesimus in love. Paul also promises to repay any debts Onesimus may have incurred or to make good on any harm caused.

But despite its brevity, this letter raises more questions than it answers. We aren't given the backstory of the harm between Philemon and Onesimus, nor are we told exactly who Onesimus is. The phrase "receive him back" has led many to assume that Onesimus was a runaway slave.[27] This gave rise to a common interpretation: Philemon owned a slave named Onesimus, who escaped—a crime that, if discovered, could result in severe beatings or, worse, death. The story goes that while on the run, Onesimus encountered Paul, who converted him to follow Jesus. Paul then writes to Philemon, urging him to welcome Onesimus back without punishment, as a brother.[28]

This was the story entertained in some of my evangelical small group discussions that glossed over the horrors of slavery, arguing that Roman slavery was *not quite like* American chattel slavery—as if anyone should condone *any form* of slavery. Some Christians love to warn about "slippery slopes," and if you ask me, this logic feels like one of them. Worse, proslavery apologists used this interpretation to argue that slavery was tolerable, even acceptable, because the New Testament does not explicitly speak against it. In fact, they pointed out, Paul sends Onesimus back into servitude, which they took as its unspoken endorsement.[29]

But a deeper reading troubles this narrative, and it's worth paying attention to. If Onesimus was indeed an escaped slave, then sending him back would have violated Deuteronomy 23:15–16, which forbids returning runaway slaves to their masters. But perhaps more striking is the fact that Paul never explicitly calls Onesimus a slave. Instead, his language is far more radical. He calls Onesimus Philemon's "brother." "Maybe this is the reason that Onesimus was separated from you for a while," Paul writes, "so that you might have him back forever—no longer as a slave but more than a slave—that is, as a dearly loved brother. He is especially a dearly loved brother to me. How much more can he become a brother to you, personally and spiritually in the Lord!" (Philem. 15–16).

Abolitionists argued that Paul's use of "slave" here was metaphorical, much like how Paul calls himself a "slave" in the greetings of some of his letters, such as in Romans, Philippians, and Titus. Some even suggested that Onesimus and Philemon were not enslaver and enslaved at all but estranged biological brothers divided by some domestic conflict, and that Paul's letter was a plea for reconciliation.[30]

But those who defended slavery read it differently. They insisted that "slave" was literal, while "brother" was nothing more than a spiritual metaphor for being "brothers in faith." They took the phrase "in the flesh" to refer to Onesimus's physical return to Philemon. And despite the outcry from abolitionists, this reading became widely accepted into the consciousness of most modern interpretations.[31]

The letter to Philemon is a reminder that interpretation is never free from bias. Whether it is seen as a story of reconciliation or a quiet endorsement of bondage depends entirely on what the reader brings to it.[32] And in the colonial era, those assumptions were deeply shaped by the institution of slavery and the needs of those in power. It's a sobering truth: Biblical interpretation has always been influenced—and at times distorted—by political and colonial forces. What we choose to see in the text often reveals more about the systems and hierarchies we're trying to preserve or dismantle than it does about the text itself.

A Kin-dom of Belonging

Empire has a way of crafting self-serving narratives, painting a picture of what's "good" and "necessary" for society. Think about how the hierarchal child-rearing methods promoted by James Dobson and his contemporaries were marketed as producing well-adjusted, happy families. The Duggars, too, offered a pristine image of a loving, close-knit Christian household. But behind those idealized images was often the reality of abuse and trauma. Jill Duggar's revelations about manipulation and deception, along with the scandals surrounding Josh Duggar, exposed the cracks in that facade.

The same distortion plays out in how American history is being rewritten. In 2023, under the leadership of Ron DeSantis, new public-school curricula were introduced in Florida suggesting that slavery had "benefits" for enslaved people, such as the development of certain skills.[33] The curricula also downplayed the violence of the Reconstruction era, implying a false equivalence between violence committed in self-defense by African Americans and violence committed against them in the form of lynchings, massacres, and political intimidation. Empire rewrites history, distorting the truth to create a more favorable narrative, one that smooths over the atrocities that lie at its foundation.

While empire paints its own pictures, Scripture offers different visions. The prophet Isaiah imagines a world remade, where humanity's role in creation is restored. He writes of a peace so profound that "the wolf will live with the lamb, and the leopard will lie down with the young goat; the calf and the young lion will feed together" (Isa. 11:6). But what strikes me is the final part, "and a little child will lead them." It's an image of a world remade, where one of the most vulnerable—a child—leads with gentleness, dignity, mutuality, and care. In this transformed creation, the ones historically overlooked and oppressed teach us the most about belonging.[34] I imagine that child not as merely symbol, but as someone real—one of the Native children buried in an unmarked grave, taken too soon. I imagine them standing barefoot, whispering the songs they were forbidden to sing, leading not with vengeance but with a quiet strength that remembers what the world tried to erase.

Jesus consistently points to children as examples of discipleship (Matt. 18:4–5; Mark 9:36–37; Luke 9:47–48). In a time when adults were seen as the sole holders of knowledge, Jesus's words were radical. He flips the script, resisting the status quo that places power in the hands of the few. In Matthew, he thanks God for revealing divine truth not to the "wise and intelligent" but to "babies" (11:25). It's a subversive declaration—that revelation comes to those on the margins, those who are dismissed.

Later, when the disciples try to scold the people bringing their children to Jesus for a blessing, he stops them, saying, "Allow the children to come to me. . . . God's kingdom belongs to people like these children" (Mark 10:14). In saying this, Jesus makes clear that God's kingdom does not belong to the ones who think they hold the keys to the divine. No, it's for the weak, the lowly, the ones the world has cast aside. The children, the women, the enslaved—God's vision of belonging is revealed to and through them.

This divine kingdom is defined by mutuality and belonging. It's a *kin-dom*, as Cuban American theologian Ada María Isasi-Díaz described it, introducing the term to challenge the hierarchical and often exclusionary language of "kingdom" and the negative connotations of traditional religious language associated with "king." The kin-dom is about gathering, not ruling. It's a space where no one is left out or marginalized. For Isasi-Díaz, the kin-dom is revealed when we build spaces where kinship, not hierarchy, is the way forward.[35]

This kin-dom is God's liberation unfolding among us; it offers a table where all are welcomed and everyone belongs. It's what Paul is pointing to in Galatians when he says, "There is neither slave nor free; nor is there male and female, for you are all one in Christ Jesus" (3:28). It's a vision of deep interconnectedness, a new creation where mutuality and equality are at the heart of God's movement in the world.

———

When my daughter was two, she broke her elbow. It happened in the simplest of ways. My husband was holding her hand at the edge of the street, ready to cross, when she suddenly bolted toward me. Feeling her tug, he instinctively tightened his grip, and our toddler fell to the ground in pain. At the time, the injury seemed minor; a small stumble surely wouldn't cause real harm. We did what parents do: We held her, rocked her, soothed her tears. But no matter what we tried, the pain didn't subside. She'd already had a difficult morning full of emotions too big for her little body. We chalked this up as an extension of that—a stubbed-toe kind of hurt that feels worse when you're already worn down.

After a short time, though, it was clear she wasn't just being emotional; something was deeply wrong. We took her to the ER, but the doctor didn't seem concerned. She brushed it off as a toddler being dramatic and sent us home with a prescription for ibuprofen. But the pain didn't leave, and the longer it lingered, the more I kept thinking, *I just want to believe her.*

And I'm so glad I did. We took her back for an x-ray that confirmed she had a fractured bone and needed a cast.

There's something about hierarchy and power that teaches us not to believe those deemed below us. When people express their suffering, we downplay it, dismissing their pain as a misunderstanding, an exaggeration of reality—based on our limited perspective. But the truth of the experience belongs to the one who bears it.

I learned that firsthand several years ago when some colleagues and I went white water rafting in the Dominican Republic during a service trip. I'm not one to chase adrenaline for the fun of it, but others in the group assured me it wasn't dangerous. So despite my nerves, I strapped on a life vest and helmet and got into the raft. At first the ride was smooth, even pleasant, until we approached our first waterfall. We were told to distribute our weight and hold on tight. Next thing I knew, I was crashing against rocks, tumbling under the white water. I was trying to figure out which way was up, but I was being tossed in too many directions to find it. After swallowing too much water in an effort to take a breath, I panicked. *This is it*, I thought. *This is how I die.*

Then hands grabbed my vest and snatched me from the current. The raft ahead of us had seen us flip and pulled over by some rocks to help those of us who had gone under. Two of us had been caught in the rapids; the others had managed to navigate the drop and swim to safety. I was distraught, shaking. Terrified to get back in the raft, I cried and begged them to find another route, but there was no other option. I had to continue with the others.

I'll never forget that day. But just as vivid as that moment in the rapids is what happened a few months later at a gathering with the same group. As we reminisced, I recalled my experience, only for someone to roll their eyes and say to the others, "It wasn't that bad." Their words stung like a slap in the face.

In a way, they were right. It wasn't that bad—*for them*. Their body hadn't been scraped against the rocks, their breath stolen by the current. And because they hadn't felt that surge of fear flood their chest, they labeled my retelling as an exaggeration.

Their minimizing my experience made me feel invisible. And that's how I've felt on several other occasions—in seminary classrooms, around the dinner table with male family members, in church settings with pastors and leaders—when I wasn't believed, when my experience was scoffed at as if I was unworthy of being taken seriously. Like the time a pastor said I was wishy-washy because I declined his offer to start and run a full-time ministry for little more than pennies a week. I was young, but I knew my worth, and in refusing, I was labeled unreliable. And that word, like a seed, found its way into future conversations, shutting doors that might have otherwise been open. It took me years to shake that lie.

I think of my white water rafting experience not because it was the most significant moment of being dismissed but because it mirrors every other time it's happened: Each one has felt like near death. And for many around the globe, it often is. Take Black mothers, who die at the highest rates in childbirth because their concerns are more likely to be dismissed. This is the weight of a medical system that, like so many others, was built on structures of racism that do not value Black lives or hear Black voices.

This is the way hierarchy works. Those with power think they get to delegitimize everyone else's experiences. And that's why part of my decolonizing work as a mother starts with the commitment to believe my daughter. I believe her when she says something hurts. I believe her when she's overwhelmed by feelings that seem insignificant to me. I want her to grow up knowing that her pain and her emotions will never be trivialized. This is how we begin to build a society of truth-tellers who know their worth. A society of kinship.

But to do this for others, I first have to do it for myself. I must work toward healing the inner child in me who once needed her pain to be believed and her voice to be heard. I listen to her, honor her, and respect her as the wise person she is. This is the work of reparenting: teaching myself to honor my emotions so I can teach my children to do the same. I remind them, and myself, that it's okay to cry, to feel sad, to be angry—to feel the full spectrum of what needs to be felt. These emotions don't scare or intimidate me anymore.

Of course, I'm not perfect. I sometimes react out of my own hurt, but I've learned that while *ruptures* in relationships are inevitable, it's the process of *repair* that matters most. Dan Siegel speaks to this in *The Whole-Brain Child*, explaining how these moments of disconnection can become opportunities for growth if followed by repair, which restores the relationship and builds resilience.[36] The moments when I have taken responsibility for my actions have drawn me closer to my children. Acknowledging my own humanity also builds trust. We foster true kinship and belonging by repairing the ruptures in our relationships.

This is why movements for justice—like #LandBack and the call for reparations—are so important. They're not just about restitution; they're about repair. They're about recognizing the ruptures caused by systems of oppression and doing the work to make things right. Like the Civil Liberties Act of 1988, which provided reparations to Japanese Americans interned during World War II. Or like in 2024 when Minnesota returned land to the Upper Sioux Community—a small step but a profound act of repair for land stolen during the US-Dakota War of 1862, when many Dakota people suffered starvation and even death due to broken treaty promises.[37] While these examples only scratch the surface, they are a necessary first step toward justice.

This is how we build a society rooted in kinship, a society where truth is honored and voices are believed. As Maslow's hierarchy of needs suggests, belonging is essential to our survival. We can't thrive alone.[38] Solidarity is about recognizing that the kin-dom is unfolding right now. It is not some far-off dream but a reality we create with each act of repair, each story honored, each life given the dignity it deserves.

Prayer of Resistance

God of Kin,

We renounce the chains of hierarchy that bind our souls, choosing instead the freedom found in mutual care. We confess the times we've lost our way in the illusion of power. Let mercy fall over us like rain, for it is here, in this tenderness, that kinship breathes. We long for our lives to be bound by the holy truth of belonging—one body, one breath, moving together in love's quiet rebellion, shaking the foundations of what was, and rising toward what can be.

We see all as equal in the kin-dom of God.

Benediction

May we walk softly, mindful of the dignity that rests in every soul, especially those the world casts aside. Let our steps be tender and our hearts open, as we tend to the beauty within each person. May our lives be a testament to a world where all are seen and nurtured, and where every life has the space to bloom in its fullest, most radiant form. We will go as kin, bound by love and dignity.

    Amen.

CHAPTER 5

Rejecting Dualism, Embracing Paradox

Invocation

Holy Paradox, we do not come grasping for certainty but seeking to make our home in mystery. We release the illusion of divisions—the false borders drawn between spirit and flesh, between sacred and ordinary. Here, in the space between knowing and unknowing, we open ourselves to the presence that lingers in both.

We release the need for either/or. We embrace the both/and.

Reflection

The White Mountain Apache people tell a story about a woman who weaves the world:

> *There is an old woman who sits at the edge of the world, weaving together all things—earth, sky, plants, and creatures. Her loom stretches beyond time itself, and with every thread she pulls, the world is mended, balanced, and made whole.*

But a trickster, the crow, watches her work with gleaming eyes. The crow is clever, filled with questions and curiosity. He flutters to the old woman and asks, "Why do you weave? The world falls apart as quickly as you mend it." She says nothing, her hands moving like the wind, steady and sure.

Crow, impatient as always, tugs at a loose thread in her tapestry. He pulls and pulls until a great tear forms, unraveling days, years, and mountains. He laughs at the chaos, certain he's proven his point. But the old woman only smiles, watching as the torn threads drift back to her loom. Slowly, she begins weaving again, more intricate, more beautiful than before. "For every thread you break," she says, "I create ten more." Crow caws in frustration, caught in the paradox: His mischief leads not to ruin but to creation.

Those who have ears let them hear.

I remember waking before dawn in my first days of tending to our farm, the quiet of the world still holding its breath. I'd make my way out to the animal pen, and they'd greet me in their own way: goats bleating, chickens clucking, the pigs nudging me for attention. From the very start, I knew this wasn't just work. There, in the rhythm of feeding, cleaning, and listening to the gentle sounds of life around me, my soul sensed a sacred truth woven in me long ago.

The revelations weren't loud, nor were they the kind of spiritual experience you'd find in a carefully curated worship space. It was in the way the soil smelled after rain, the sun stretching across the hill, the trust the animals placed in me. I began to remember a fundamental truth. Holiness isn't something set apart for specific times or places; it's everywhere, knit into the very fabric of the ordinary.

These mornings on the farm always carried me back to Abuela's kitchen, where I'd watch her move with such ease through the familiar rhythms of preparing a meal. No recipes, just instincts honed over decades guiding her hands. While the air was thick with the scent of beans simmering on the stove, she'd tell me stories of our ancestors: their struggles, their triumphs, and how they used the land not just for sustenance but also to honor their roots.

It was in those moments, surrounded by the smells of the earth, where the holy and the ordinary first collided for me. Her cooking, her stories, the way she moved through her life, everything was connected. To her, the sacred wasn't something you waited for in a church or in a ritual, it was in the everyday, in the way you lived and breathed and moved through the world.

————

It wasn't until I found myself in the evangelical church that the lines between the sacred and the secular started to be drawn. There I was taught, perhaps even without intention, that God could only be encountered in curated places, in worship sessions or in dimly lit rooms—the quiet, controlled spaces of an open Bible and closed doors.

And sure, I've felt God's nearness in those moments. But something inside of me began to fracture when I realized I was searching for God there alone, as though divinity could only be encountered when someone else had crafted the moment. The more I tried to draw close, the more God seemed to drift beyond reach. Holiness became something I had to enter rather than something I carried.

This false divide between the sacred and the secular permeates much of Christian thought. It's the belief that God is present here but not there, moving among certain people or places, as if the Spirit can be boxed into or absent from specific corners of our lives. This mindset extends beyond buildings or songs. It's an entire way of categorizing our faith: Some of us are saved and others are lost; there are saints and sinners, the elect and the doomed. This is a theology that shaped me once, the Calvinist belief that God draws near to a few and turns away from the rest. It clings to verses on predestination while ignoring the chorus of Scripture that speaks of a love beyond measure.

But this dualism doesn't stay within the walls of the church. The split between mind and body, good and evil, and beauty and shame is a way of seeing the world that makes life feel neater, less uncertain. But in this ease, we sacrifice the vast spectrum that exists between extremes, and the richness of life's in-between. We trade depth for simplicity, reducing our neighbor to something digestible instead of embracing the wildness of who they are.

For many of us, this dualistic thinking is so ingrained that we don't even notice it, let alone question it. But Christianity itself refuses to fit into these categories. It's a religion of paradoxes that says that the first shall be last, that power is made perfect in weakness, that life comes through death. Things that should cancel each other out instead intertwine and persist, like vines twisting and thriving in places where they shouldn't be able to grow and yet they do.

Christianity, at its essence, is an invitation into the mystery of God who is present in all things—unexpected, interwoven, and always defying the limits we try to place on the divine presence.

How Did We Get Here?

Dualism has shaped our understanding of ourselves and of the world for centuries. From ancient Greek philosophers like Plato to modern thinkers like René Descartes, a worldview emerged that split mind from body, reason from emotion, and spirit from flesh.

Plato believed the world we see and touch is mere illusion, that true reality exists in the realm of ideas and reason.[1] He viewed the body as nothing more than a prison for the soul or the mind, which he considered the truest self. Life's purpose, then, was to transcend the physical, allowing the soul to free itself from the body. This mindset not only elevated thought above flesh, intellect above feeling, and reason above experience, it also laid the foundation for a psychology and culture obsessed with mastery and control.[2] To rule oneself was paramount, a concept that would later prove essential to empire.

Plato's sense of self was defined by distinctions; he was not barbarian, not woman, not animal. This divided the world into rigid opposites: man versus woman, self versus other. In this framework opposites don't complement, like yin and yang, but are locked in a struggle where one must always dominate the other. This way of thinking objectifies and detaches, making tension an enemy and choosing hierarchy over harmony. It fractures instead of integrates, severing us from the world, from each other, even from our own wholeness.

But what if these tensions weren't meant to be subdued? What if mind and body, reason and feeling are not at war but in relationship? What if wisdom isn't about escape but embrace, a rhythm where opposites don't compete but complete?

Aristotle, Plato's student, had his own take on dualism. He rejected Plato's strict mind-body divide but still saw hierarchies as woven into the fabric of the universe itself.[3] For him, there were rulers and the ruled, masters and slaves. He argued that some people were naturally born to dominate, while others were born to be subjugated. Aristotle viewed women as inherently inferior and destined to be ruled by men.[4]

These hierarchies became the scaffolding for much of Western thought and paved the way for the Scientific Revolution, during which thinkers like Descartes divided the world even further. Descartes famously declared, "I think, therefore I am." To him, the mind was the seat of certainty, while the body—a site of instincts, sensations, and unpredictability—couldn't be trusted. This split, known as Cartesian dualism, echoed Plato's philosophy, elevating reason and dismissing the physical.[5] But Descartes carved out a distinction that was more scientific than spiritual, seeing the body as a machine bound by the rigid laws of nature. He left behind a world of cold, material objects to be studied and the mind and the soul in a separate, untouchable realm.

Cartesian dualism profoundly shaped the Enlightenment, a period when Western thinkers put reason on a pedestal. European colonizers, armed with this worldview, saw themselves as the pinnacle of rationality and intellect. Indigenous peoples, they claimed, were controlled by their bodies and instincts and therefore "less human." Christian theologians like Thomas Aquinas sanctified these hierarchies by reinterpreting them through a religious lens, cementing a belief in the superiority of European rationality. Figures like Juan Ginés de Sepúlveda, a Spanish theologian, used these ideas to defend Spain's right to enslave Indigenous peoples.[6]

The Renaissance, with its revival of Greek culture and thought, spread these ideas further. From this era emerged the Reformation, sending shockwaves through every facet of society. As the modern nation-state emerged, Christianity became deeply intertwined with political power. This was different from the earlier marriage of Christianity and empire under Constantine; now, Christianity was infused with the philosophical ideas of Plato and Aristotle, blending faith with the logic of ancient Greek thought.[7]

Plato's belief in the soul's immortality and separation from the body also influenced theologians like Augustine, who argued that if God is pure goodness, then God cannot be associated with the physical world, which he saw as tainted by evil.[8] The body, the earth, the material world became a site of suspicion, prone to sin and corruption. This split laid the groundwork for empire by reinforcing the concept of a negative "other." Christianity, especially in its imperial alignments, has long relied on this "other" to define itself, associating salvation with separation—from the body, from earthly desires, and ultimately from certain groups of people deemed inferior, impure, or sinful—to decide who belongs and who doesn't.

This plays into the way Western Christian theology centers the sanctified self over the collective—framing spirituality as an

individual possession rather than a shared experience. It emphasizes a personal relationship with God, as if the divine resides
primarily "in our hearts." But early Christianity wasn't about
isolated personal salvation, it was about the whole. The lives of
early Jesus followers were bound together, shaped by the act of
feeding and sheltering, by the way they held one another's suffering as their own. It was embodied and communal, not confined
to the private spaces of the soul.

The shift toward personal salvation gained momentum during
the Protestant Reformation. Scripture, once read in community,
was placed into individual hands, and interpretation became a
private endeavor. The Spirit, once sought in the gathered body,
became something to be deciphered alone. And so, the church,
meant to be a people, became a scattering of separate souls, each
with their own claim to truth.

Itinerant preachers in North America deepened this divide. More
and more, people entrusted a single authoritative figure over a community to receive the Word of the Lord.[9] The more charismatic the
preacher, the larger the crowds they drew. Success was measured in
numbers, and faith became less about the collective transformation
of society and more about the tallying of saved souls.

But this wasn't just a theological shift; it was a political one
that aligned religious authority and salvation with emerging ideas
of individualism, nationhood, and power. Colonizers and revolu-
tionaries saw themselves as defenders of liberty, believing it was
their Christian duty to fight for the birth of a new nation. But
their concept of liberty prioritized individual rights over collective
responsibility. Even as they rejected the rule of European mon-
archs, they denied that same freedom to the Indigenous peoples
whose land they seized and the enslaved Africans whose bodies
they exploited. The settlers cast themselves as the sanctified, the
enlightened, while Indigenous peoples and the enslaved became
the "other," evidence of all they believed themselves to have tran-
scended. This framework helped fuel the United States' governing

bodies and laid the foundation for the religious, political, and social structures that would shape the country's future.[10] And the churches that emerged from this period? They were built on this same dualism: liberation for the few, subjugation for the rest.

Letting Our Light Shine?

I remember the way we used to sing "This Little Light of Mine" in catechism class. We'd hold our index fingers up high like tiny flames, and declare with everything in us, "Hide it under a bushel? No!" And with even more passion, "Don't let Satan blow it out! I'm gonna let it shine!" For us, the message was clear as day: God is not present in the darkness. For so much of my early faith, that's what salvation meant. Once lost in the dark, I had become a child of light. And no words shaped that understanding more than the beginning of the Gospel of John:

> What came into being
>> through the Word was life,
>> and the life was the light for all people.
> The light shines in the darkness,
>> and the darkness doesn't extinguish the light. (1:3–5)

The poetry of John has stirred hearts for centuries, and I was no exception. I was captivated by this image of Jesus—the Word, the light—piercing through the dark. I have always loved language, the way a single word can hold something so vast. But looking back, I see how these words in all their poetic beauty might have contributed to a way of seeing the world I am now trying to dismantle.

I now see the subtle dualism ingrained in the teachings of my youth. How by raising our index fingers high we were learning something deeper than a melody—we were being formed to see the world in binaries, a stark division between believers and nonbelievers, saved and lost. What seemed innocent enough in childhood wasn't harmless at all.

I was taught to see darkness only as absence. As something empty, something to fear. No one ever told me that darkness is where seeds are buried before they bloom. That it is the womb of creation. That before God said, *Let there be light*, the Spirit was already there, hovering over the deep.

What if we have spent so much time trying to escape the dark that we have missed the God who dwells within it?

The problem isn't necessarily how John understood salvation or even the language in the Gospel itself; rather, the problem springs from how Greek philosophy has shaped our thinking and led us to read dualism into the Bible, missing the paradox and mystery of the Word. Such enmeshment doesn't just shape doctrine, it shapes how we encounter God.

This binary mindset was weaponized to rationalize colonial and missionary efforts to bring the "light of the gospel" to the so-called "heathen" in the non-Western world.[11] The darkness wasn't just metaphorical anymore—it represented a people, a geography, a skin. The Word became flesh, but in the hands of empire, the message became something that fractured us instead of knitting us together.

This dualistic framework strips away the richness of the human experience, reducing whole people to symbols, stereotypes, or monoliths. Frantz Fanon reminds us that the erasure of our complexity is empire's greatest theft. He speaks of how colonialism erodes identity, reducing People of Color to roles that serve its narrative—always "the native," always "the oppressed," as if our existence is static, singular. But we are not one thing. We carry worlds within us, histories and futures colliding in every breath. We must reclaim our right to nuance, to reject the binaries empire imposes.[12]

To essentialize people is an act of violence. It severs the sacred chaos of who we are from our bodies and our histories. We are complexity incarnate—uncontainable, defiant in our wholeness, unyielding in our joy, grief, and contradictions. To know ourselves truly, we must surrender the myth of simplicity and sit with the beauty of our depths. We must remember that we are spirit *and* we are flesh.

This understanding mirrors a deeper truth found in the Hebrew scriptures, which doesn't speak of a soul severed from a body. While Jewish thought is diverse, much of the tradition views the human being as an integrated whole—flesh and spirit woven together, inseperable. So when John's Gospel declares that the Word became flesh in Jesus (1:14), this isn't just theological; it is radical. It declares that the body isn't incidental to faith but essential. Jesus's incarnation wasn't a concession to our physical existence; it was a declaration of its sacredness.

And the resurrection? It wasn't just the triumph of a soul; it was the return and restoration of a body, scarred and breathing. This is a defiance of the Greek notion that death was a release from the material world. Instead, it declared that bodies—this very skin, this very breath—carry meaning beyond the grave. The early Christian story refused the hierarchical dualism that pits body against soul, that names one eternal and the other disposable. Instead, it entwined word and flesh, spirit and sinew, light and dark.

Ambivalence Sets Us Free

I've come to realize something important since leaving a spiritual community bound by rigid borders and strict intellectual limits: Leaving can be as daunting as staying. It's stifling to have watchful eyes and ears keeping you from straying too far, but it can be equally debilitating when your spiritual territory isn't clearly mapped out. There's a strange safety when the lines between right and wrong, good and evil, us and them are clear. Certainty drapes over you like fog, obscuring the labor of discernment. When I knew what Bible translation to read, what songs to sing, what voices to trust, the hard work of faith had already been done for me, and I found comfort in its simplicity. Even if it kept me captive.

But this simplicity does more than restrict us, it limits our ability to love fully. It's easy to love a neighbor whose story doesn't challenge yours, whose existence is easily digestible. The black-and-white world keeps us from the complexity of everyday life and the tension of true faith—the kind that asks us to sit in uncertainty, to embrace contradiction, and to hold the wildness of others with grace and nuance, trusting that God dwells there too.

The illusion of certainty masquerades as spirituality, but the real stuff is found in the messy middle—in the ambiguity, the doubt, *the ambivalence.* They're not just tolerated but held as sacred. Spirituality that denies these freedoms is nothing more than subjugation. And subjugation, whether spiritual or political, thrives on rigid binaries and false assurance that one is either fully in or fully out, wholly right or wholly wrong. But reality, especially under systems of power, is rarely that simple.

Homi Bhabha speaks of this tension in the relationship between the colonizer and the colonized, describing it as ambivalent. This relationship is never a clean opposition, nor is it ever straightforward. The colonized are neither just passive victims nor rebellious subjects. Instead, they live in a tangled middle, caught in a complex dance of resistance and compliance.[13] Sometimes resistance looks like mimicry, which is an imitating of the oppressor in ways that mock and subvert them. As Bhabha explains, it destabilizes their authority, reflecting back the injustice of the system while exposing its cracks.[14] This is the unpredictable, messy work of survival. But perhaps that is its power. To live in the in-between is to carry the ability to disrupt even the strongest empires through the slow, quiet undoing of the narratives that uphold them.

You can see this disruption in the story of the poor widow in Mark 12:41–44. How many sermons have focused on her parting with two small coins as the gold standard of generosity, a model of sacrificial giving? They tell us she gave all she had, and so we should do the same. But what if we've been reading it all wrong? What if there's something deeper beneath the surface, something we weren't taught to see?

In the first-century world, widows were among the most marginalized people groups. Without a husband or male protector, they occupied a precarious place in both the Jewish community and the Roman imperial system. Yet in her offering, this widow does something quietly subversive; she gives everything, not just in obedience to Torah but in a way that mirrors the public displays of wealth by the imperial elite. Her action isn't merely about faith but also mimics the pageantry of the wealthy.

This widow, often viewed as meek and powerless, performs a notable act reminiscent of the rich, who declared their gifts in public. Yet she does so from her poverty. In an act of embodied resistance, she rejects the false divisions between the sacred and the profane, the powerful and the powerless. By offering all she has to a temple system complicit in her oppression, the widow exposes its failure to care for the vulnerable. And here's the twist: Widows like her often relied on the temple's redistribution of funds to survive. In essence, she gives everything to the institution that exploits her, knowing she'll get it right back. This is not an act of unquestioning loyalty but a quiet, subversive act, exposing the empire's illusion of power. Because the body—the material, the flesh—is not something to be discarded or exploited. Even those the world casts aside are sacred, potent, and capable of a resistance that those in power will never comprehend.

In the broader context of Mark, we see Jesus entering Jerusalem in a "triumphal entry" that mimics Roman imperial processions. He overturns tables in the temple, condemning its exploitation. The widow's act reflects this critique. Jesus praises her not to encourage emulation but to call his disciples to notice her defiance— a resistance so subtle it almost goes unnoticed.

The widow invites us to reimagine resistance. It is not always loud or visible but often quiet, cunning, and deeply profound. She reminds us that even in the face of exploitation, there are ways to claim dignity and speak truth, even if it's in a language only the oppressed can hear.

The widow's defiance calls to mind another act of quiet subversion, one that unfolds not in the temple but by the water's edge. Jesus tells Peter to pay the temple tax, not from his own pocket but with a coin pulled from the mouth of a fish. The temple tax was a symbol of empire's grip on faith, a demand for allegiance wrapped in ritual. But in this story, the tax is paid as a declaration of divine abundance. The coin comes not from the toil or scarcity of empire but from creation itself—God's provision, unbent by human systems.

In this way, Jesus participates in the system only to subvert it and expose its fragility: A kingdom that has to borrow from the waters and the wild to assert its authority has no real authority at all. And maybe that's what we're called to do—to live in a way that reveals empire's emptiness while trusting in the abundance of a kin-dom that cannot be taxed or taken.

The Case for Harmony

The meeting ground between the self and the other need not be a battlefield, though that's how empires throughout history have framed it, often invoking the divine to justify their atrocities. From ancient emperors to modern missionaries, relationships between self and other have been drawn in rigid lines, with conquest and domination seemingly ordained by the gods. "It must be this way now," they say, "because the divine has willed it from the beginning."

When we believe the divine wills something absolutely, we stop wrestling with the complexity of the world. It's how dualism still thrives in religious spaces today. I've felt it in many church settings—the pressure to see my own will as something to be set aside, to understand my desires as inherently in conflict with God's. What I wanted, thought, or felt was always considered at odds with the divine. It wasn't a both/and but an either/or. Either God was at work or I was. This set up a relentless internal tension, not just with God but with myself.

But the more I immersed myself in Scripture, the more I saw that God isn't at war with humanity. The stories we find there aren't about a battle of wills but about a sacred dance—about God and humans moving together in harmony, creating something holy. This reframing shifted something deep within me, reminding me that the religious life isn't a struggle for control but a movement of grace and love.

In Eastern cultures, paradox is something to be embraced, not resolved. The philosophy of yin and yang teaches us to understand duality as something holistic and dynamic, a living relationship. Opposing forces, instead of being in conflict, exist in a kind of conversation, transforming and balancing each other under different conditions, each one holding a piece of its opposite.[15] Winter contains the seed of summer, just as darkness holds the promise of light. These elements live in a constant ebb and flow, creating a union that's both tension and harmony. Perhaps this is what our will and God's will are like—not enemies, but companions in the fullness of life.

It's a shame we've lost this understanding in the West, where we feel compelled to reconcile paradox, to make one right and the other wrong. But isn't our faith built on paradox? Jesus, human and divine. Mary, virgin and mother. God, three and one. Western theology has spilled so much ink trying to resolve these mysteries, but perhaps they are not meant to be solved. Perhaps we are invited to hold in our hearts what we can't fully grasp with our minds.

Mystery and paradox are the way of faith, yet we have been conditioned to believe that living in tension is something that needs to be reconciled. But spiritual growth often looks like confronting our contradictions, especially the ones that live in us—our shadow selves, the parts of us we would rather not face. I've long been on a journey of decolonizing, of working to free myself from the systems of Western imperialism. Even so, when I need diapers in a pinch, I turn to Amazon for the convenience, fully aware that my choice feeds a system that exploits workers and the earth. We all live in such contradictions because there is no perfect way to do this work. We must constantly check ourselves against these systems with integrity and refuse to put limits on others that we have yet to put on ourselves.

Here's where a profound paradox lies: The closer we get to Divine Light, the more clearly we see our own shadows, and this too is grace. Father Richard Rohr reminds us that "Sin and shadow are not the same. We were so encouraged to avoid sin that many of us instead avoided facing our shadow."[16] It's the spiritually mature, Rohr says, who have learned to face their shadows, leaving less to hide or project onto the world. This ongoing, painful, beautiful work is what keeps us from making the "other" our enemy. It draws us into the sacred practice of holding both light and shadow, both self and other in the tension of love. The more we hold that tension, the more room we make for God.

So perhaps the path to our collective liberation begins with tending to the shadows within ourselves with a quiet curiosity. This is the hardest and most important work I face as a mother, teaching my young child to understand her emotions without labeling them "good" or "bad." Anger, sadness, and frustration are not sins to be purged but signals of our humanity, of something deeper stirring within us. A contemplative soul is willing to look inward first, to pay attention to what's going on inside. Only then can we look outward, can we see the "other" in our midst. Only then can we create harmony where there is division. As Rohr says, "Whole people see and create wholeness wherever they go; split people see and create splits in everything and everybody."[17]

I think of the widow. The story begins with Jesus sitting down, watching the crowd (Mark 12:41). I'm not sure what he was looking for, but the widow captures his attention. When he sees what she has done, he calls the disciples over and urges them to see her too.

But notice that Jesus doesn't command, "Do what she does," as the sermons on sacrificial giving might insist. No, what I hear is something simpler yet more profound: *Look at this woman.* It's not a guilt trip or a demand. It's an invitation to pay attention—to her, the one no one else thought to notice, the one many labeled "other."

We are liberated when we're able to notice the stirrings of life happening inside us and out, and in the spaces in-between where we don't know to look. As my friend Shannan Martin once wrote, "This world is crying out for belonging, but we'll get there only if we're willing to stay watchful."[18]

Prayer of Resistance

God of Paradox,

We reject the lie of separation and cast off the chains of dualism. We confess the moments we failed to see the "other" as ourselves. In forgiveness, we are set free, gently holding the complexity of our shared humanity. Our hearts grow wide enough to cradle the world's harmony. With each breath, may we inhale the love that binds us—united, unbroken, unashamed.

We acknowledge that all are woven together in the sacred fabric of being.

Benediction

May we journey through life not in search of answers but in pursuit of deeper questions. We lay down the fear of contradiction, and in its place we hold the sacred wisdom found in tension. In this space, we—both the lost and the found, both the broken and the whole—learn. We embrace paradox, for it is here that we find the fullness of life.

Amen.

CHAPTER 6

Rejecting Hustle, Embracing Slowness

Invocation

Embodied Presence, remind us of the sacred value of our bodies.
In a world that demands we produce, consume, and repeat, we
choose to pause. To breathe. To listen. To remember that we were
not made for exhaustion, but for embodiment, wonder, and rest.

*We are here to reclaim our time, our energy, and our right to
simply be.*

Reflection

There's a story told about a Mexican fisherman:

> *A businessman is vacationing in a small coastal village when
> he comes across a fisherman who has just returned with his
> daily catch. The businessman asks the fisherman how long
> it took him to catch the fish, and the fisherman replies that it
> took him only a short while. Surprised, the businessman asks
> why he doesn't fish longer and catch more. The fisherman*

explains that the small catch is enough to feed his family and that the rest of his day is spent relaxing, playing with his children, and enjoying life.

The businessman tells the fisherman that if he spends more time fishing, he could catch more fish, make more money, buy a bigger boat to catch even more fish, and start a fishing company. After the company grows, the fisherman could move to a big city, manage a fleet of boats, and earn millions.

The fisherman asks how long this would take. The businessman estimates it might take fifteen to twenty years. The fisherman then asks what he would do after all this hard work. The businessman responds that he could retire, move to a quiet village, fish for pleasure, relax, spend time with his family, and enjoy his life. The fisherman smiles and says, "Isn't that what I am doing now?"

Those who have ears let them hear.

When I think of being in my body as a child, a flood of memories surface. I remember rollerblading under the Miami sun at Tropical Park, the heat wrapping around me like a second skin. I remember diving under water at Venetian Pool, my body the smell of chlorine and summer. I think of swinging so high at the playground that I'd float for a few seconds, suspended in the sky, before gravity pulled me back down to the earth. Or hanging upside down from the monkey bars, the blood rushing to my head with a force that made the world spin.

There are other memories too, memories etched into the marrow of my being. Of afternoons spent nestled in Abuela Flora's lap, my head resting against her chest. We breathed together, slow and heavy, as her hands traced gentle patterns down my back, sending goosebumps to the surface of my skin. In her arms, I felt the fullness of my humanity. I felt precious. I felt loved. There was strength and fragility, safety and belonging. It was in those moments, skin against skin, that I learned what it meant to be truly alive in my body.

Abuela Flora died when I was in elementary school. She died of old age at home surrounded by family, but the truth is she hadn't arrived at old age without scars. Several failed suicide attempts marked her path, though no one ever told me about them then. As a child, I was only told she was "sick" when she ended up in the hospital, unaware that there were days—sometimes just before or after our moments of tenderness in her recliner—when she had tried to end her own life. The colonial wounds she carried were too deep to bear. The mental anguish of being physically distant from her island, her people, wore on her like an invisible weight.

Colonialism carves its scars into flesh and spirit alike. It's easy to forget that the same hands that nurture us also sometimes carry the weight of generational trauma, of displacement, of a history that tried to steal one's sense of belonging. Abuela bore these scars from empire's violence, wounds that nearly took her life. And yet, in her arms, I felt only love. The tension between the suffering she carried and the care she gave is the paradox at the heart of empire's legacy.

———

Despite our vast differences, there is one thing every person on this planet shares: the experience of having a body. We are all embodied beings, living in skin that holds both joy and pain.

Yet our experiences within our bodies are anything but the same. Empire has always been in the business of assigning value to differences, constructing systems around what it deems "ideal." But that ideal? It's always shifting in order to fit the needs of power. There was a time when larger bodies weren't shamed but rather were considered signs of wealth and status. The concept of race has never been static either. Irish, Polish, and Italian immigrants, for example, weren't always considered white in America, until the lines shifted to preserve a certain social order.[1]

Today, the body that empire prizes is typically white, male, able-bodied, and straight. The US Constitution was written with this body in mind. When the Bill of Rights was signed, the right to vote and participate in democracy was reserved for a small group, excluding even white men with disabilities.[2]

In the Roman world, the ideal body—muscular, enduring, disciplined—was no private thing. Physical strength and vitality were demands of the state, woven into its military, land, and social ideals. A man's body was not his own but a resource to be exploited for empire's collective power and prosperity. The state needed strong bodies to expand its borders, to labor in its fields, to uphold its hierarchy.

Those who didn't meet this ideal—the enslaved, women, foreigners—were pushed to the margins, seen as inherently weaker and less valuable. This exclusion reinforced who was worthy and who wasn't—a legacy that carried forward, shaping modern systems that also use bodies to uphold a specific order, a specific ideal.

Since empire has always been about control, the worth of a body is determined by its ability to serve that control. And those whose bodies don't fit into empire's mold? They're left to navigate the pain of living in bodies that are targeted for exploitation.

The Colonized Body

If you want to understand the legacy of colonialism, you only have to look at what it has done to living, breathing human bodies. It's where the ideologies play out, where the pain becomes tangible.

Since the eighteenth century, Western societies have tried to manipulate human life through various institutions, such as hospitals, prisons, and schools. They've treated the body as something separate from the self, something to be controlled, improved, or "cured" of whatever empire has deemed unacceptable. And they've often claimed these interventions were a supposed benefit of colonization.[3]

In the nineteenth century, agencies experimented on the bodies of enslaved people without their consent. These experiments were meant to advance the goals of researchers—and benefit white society as a whole—with little regard for the well-being of the people involved. For example, J. Marion Sims, known as the "father of gynecology," performed painful, invasive surgeries on enslaved Black women, without anesthesia.[4]

This pattern of medical abuse persisted. In the Tuskegee Syphilis Study, African American men infected with syphilis were misled for decades by government researchers who denied them treatment under the pretense of free health care. Similarly, Indigenous women in the 1960s and '70s were coerced into sterilization procedures, their reproductive rights stripped away in the name of "public health."[5] Historically, white American policymakers have ignored the health of marginalized communities while using the resulting high rates of illness and death to justify discrimination, like segregation or immigration restrictions. Colonial governments have quarantined migrant populations for inspection and used prisons to exploit racialized groups through forced labor or other colonizing purposes.

Because colonialism is so deeply centered on controlling bodies, it's not something that ends when countries declare independence or sign treaties. It lingers in our institutions, our laws, and our health care systems, taking on new forms and strategies. But another truth persists: There are those who resist, who refuse to let this legacy go unanswered.

In the 1970s, the Black Panther Party began a quiet, revolutionary act of healing, challenging a health care system that dismissed Black suffering. Sickle cell anemia, a disease that warps blood cells into hard crescents, was weighing heavily on Black communities but being ignored by white doctors and researchers.

So the Panthers took healing into their own hands, opening free clinics across the country for those who were used to being turned away. They tested people for the disease and educated them, making health care a communal act and serving as a radical reminder that Black bodies were sacred, worthy of reverence. Through their actions, they did more than just treat a disease: they resisted a system that sought to erase them by reclaiming the right to be whole.

Blessed Are the Disabled

Not long after beginning his ministry, Jesus gathers a crowd and begins to teach them what we now call the Beatitudes, words that have resonated deeply with many Christians. He starts with "Blessed are the poor in spirit, for theirs is the kingdom of heaven" (Matt. 5:3 NIV). That one verse, as small as it is, has been unraveled and reinterpreted in a thousand ways. Some believe he is addressing spiritual poverty or a kind of deep despair, as seen in the Common English Bible translation "happy are people who are hopeless." Others hear it as Jesus speaking to the financially poor. The Greek word for "poor" here paints an image of a person bent low, crouching and cowering, completely destitute. The different ways this verse is understood speaks to the nature of language and how words carry meaning that's shaped by culture and context as much as by the speaker.

My friend Elizabeth Staszak, a disabled scholar, takes a close look at Jesus's audience. Just before the Sermon on the Mount, Jesus has been healing people—those with diseases, those in chronic pain, those possessed by demons, epileptics, the paralyzed (Matt. 4:24). Large crowds followed him, the text says, and when he saw them, he went up a mountain and began to teach. *This* is the context behind Jesus's teaching, *this* crowd—the sick, disabled, and spiritually oppressed. Staszak reminds us that Jesus is speaking directly to those who are social outcasts, "dishonored for their status as visibly broken." He recognizes not only the visible disabilities but also "the invisible barriers set up against them by society."[6]

114

Jesus is likely among visibly and invisibly disabled people when he declares, "Blessed are the poor in spirit." During a time when disability was seen as a literal curse, Jesus says "blessed." Blessed are those who are crouching and cowering because society has cast them out. These are the people for whom the kin-dom of heaven is reserved—the ones on the lower rungs of society's ladder, the ones the world has tried to forget.

————

Ableism, like racism, sexism, heterosexism, classism, and all the other structures of violence that fracture our world, is a system that disadvantages groups of people with disabilities. But ableism impacts anyone with a body or a mind, diminishing our humanity by constructing hierarchies of worth rooted in narrow ideas of what is normal, intelligent, or desirable.[7] It deems certain bodies and minds less worthy, creating a divide between who gets to belong and who does not based on our ability to adequately produce (and reproduce), excel, and conform to certain behaviors.

Disability is not simply a medical or physical condition; it is shaped by the society we live in, by the forces of labor and the relentless demands of capitalism. It goes back to when our ancestors were forced into wage labor and bodies were judged by how well they could function. The more people produced, the faster they moved, the more valuable they became. And those who couldn't meet these demands—the deaf, the blind, those with different minds and bodies—the world didn't just ignore them but refused to make space for them.[8] They were erased from the labor market, treated as problems to be solved rather than people deserving of care and belonging.

Our bodies cry out for rest. But a majority of people today can't afford the time for this. We go to work sick and push through pain. We do this not just because we lack guaranteed sick leave or family leave but because we've been taught that our worth is in our work. We've internalized the lie that if we stop producing, we are somehow less human. Many of us cling to work to soothe the fear that somehow we don't measure up.[9] In an ableist society, only those who are productive are seen as deserving of respect, dignity, and protection.

Some of us live with pain. Many need accommodations that are so simple, like a ramp instead of stairs. Yet even these small adjustments are seen as too much, as though the world resists any movement toward accessibility because doing so would mean recognizing the humanity in all of us, not just the fastest, strongest, or most efficient. And those who fall behind aren't just left behind but judged—labeled lazy, less deserving of care or love. Ableism doesn't need a diagnosis to work its violence. It's "ready to sweep up any body that seems to be faltering."[10]

For so long, disability has been weaponized to justify oppressing people, and it has never existed in isolation. Europeans called Black and Indigenous people mentally inferior, using that as a reason to enslave and colonize them. Women were told they were too weak, too irrational to claim the right to vote or lead. Ableism has been used as a tool for maintaining other forms of inequality, a way to strip dignity and worth from those who have always belonged. This is because at its core ableism is about more than disability. It's about who gets to be seen as fully human.

The Commodified Body

As colonial America took shape, something emerged alongside it: a way of life so powerful that it would fundamentally alter global dynamics and reshape how we perceive ourselves.

Positioned within the Atlantic basin, European settlers in North America were able to control the flow of gold and silver extracted through the labor of enslaved Black and Indigenous people. That control consolidated wealth in the hands of the few. Western Europe rose to prominence in this new world order, becoming the epicenter of a vast, new system relentless in its hunger to claim new resources, exploit new markets, and deepen wealth. Peruvian sociologist Aníbal Quijano speaks of this shift as one in which all forms of labor, production, and exploitation were drawn together and organized under a new pattern of power: capitalism.[11]

Capitalism is a system of power in which the pursuit of profit reigns supreme. It organizes labor, production, and resources into a single engine driven by the demands of capital, privileging those who own and control wealth. It's not just an economic structure but a way of life, one that commodifies everything it touches, from land to human beings, reducing value to what can be bought, sold, or exploited.

At its heart, capitalism is a story of investment and expectation —money spent with a promise of return. In capitalism's early days, this return was born out of long-distance trade, which carried not just goods but the bones of entire peoples. Cotton became its lifeblood, coursing through the veins of both national and global economies.[12] We cannot tell the story of the modern world without tracing it back to the cotton factories, the ports, and most of all the plantations of the eighteenth and nineteenth centuries, where slavery fueled the machine of profit. Slavery was a system deliberately built to turn humans into commodities for the world market. Thus, capitalism and imperialism became intertwined, each feeding the other.[13]

Every form of labor—from enslaved people toiling in the fields to salaried people working in offices—became a thread in a single global fabric. There was a new way of ordering the world, and race emerged as a way of categorizing people. Suddenly, whiteness stood at the top, wearing salary, authority, and privilege like a crown.[14]

Capitalism remains embedded in the structures of our world, moving invisibly beneath the surface. It is so ingrained in our global reality that we can easily forget it's there. Yet this system of power still decides who has access to wealth and who holds power. It shapes the air we breathe, the spaces we inhabit, the structures that tell us what bodies matter.

As European states built their overseas empires, the United States constructed its own, one less formal but no less real. In the Pacific, in Latin America, it planted its stakes, carving out territories that stretched far beyond its borders. Factories began to sprout in places like Mexico and Asia, where labor was cheaper, more vulnerable, and often young. The hands of girls—too young to vote, too young to marry—stitched together the wealth of the West in factories run by companies like Nike and Gap.

The injustice is plain. Capitalism, in its global expansion, found a partner in patriarchy. Women—especially young women—are underpaid and unprotected. They're worked until there's no more profit to wring from them. Their bodies are folded into the machinery of capitalism, and when demand goes away, they're discarded like faulty equipment.[15] This system has made some so rich that they defend it as sacred.

Empire tells us that the exploited bear the blame for their own suffering. Corporations insist that capitalism thrives because it's righteous, that inequality and devastation aren't failures but necessary costs. It's a comforting lie. But if we're honest, we know that every ounce of wealth in one hand is weighed by the loss in another. This is the truth we're called to face.

The Paradox of Wage Labor

They came across the sea, thousands of Chinese men, carrying with them the weight of homes left behind and the hope of a new beginning. But they didn't know that when they set foot on this land, they'd be met with work that broke the body, stripped it of breath, and left little but exhaustion and ache.

In the West, where railroads twisted through mountains and desert, Chinese workers were paid a pittance to take on the jobs no one else would touch. The blasts of dynamite, the backbreaking lifting and hauling—they endured it all, only to be given scraps in return. They were housed in tents that barely held against the cold, fed food unfit for anyone's table, and paid less than the others, always less. And one day they'd had enough.

In the summer of 1867, thousands of Chinese workers laid down their tools and demanded what was owed to them: fair pay, a workday with dignity. They knew the risk but refused to be silent. For a week, they held firm, their bodies a wall of defiance. Though their demands were never fully met, their resistance was a fire. In a world that saw them as expendable, they reminded us all that no one should be asked to surrender their humanity for another's ambition.

———

Wage labor presents a paradox. There is, on the surface, freedom—the freedom to choose whom to work for, to step in and out of employment as one pleases. But beneath that thin veil of choice, capitalism makes it nearly impossible to survive without laboring for a paycheck. The options are few, and the control that employers exert over workers is vast. People describe it as "forced labor," and that's not rhetorical. When the alternative to wage labor is homelessness, starvation, or worse, how much choice does a person truly have? And in a wage-labor system, there is a class of people whose survival depends on the labor of others, while another class is systematically excluded.[16]

Under this kind of labor, time is regimented, the body something to be optimized. This was evident in the early factories of the Industrial Revolution, where workers were forced to work at a relentless pace.[17] And there's a deeper trap. Wage laborers are unable to produce what they need to survive, forcing them to purchase the very goods and services their own labor generates. This dependency locks them into a cycle where their wages are used to sustain the system that keeps them in a relentless loop of dependence and extraction, one that keeps turning, generation after generation.[18]

Capitalism altered not just our economy but also our relationship with time. As factories and cotton mills became the lifeblood of production, owners sought to stretch their machines and their workers to the limits. Work hours grew longer, more rigid, in a bid to extract every last ounce of efficiency. In the eighteenth century, labor became tied to the clock in a way that transformed time into something to be owned, manipulated. Employers would set clocks forward in the morning and back at night, stealing minutes, hours—lives—in an effort to maximize output. Time itself became a battleground. And by the end of the century, clocks and watches had become symbols of control, so much so that the government even tried taxing them.[19]

And so, the divide between work and nonwork began to sharpen. It was no longer about laboring and resting as the body or season called for. Instead, factory owners closed their doors during distinct holiday periods, not out of generosity but because it was easier to shut everything down than to deal with scattered absences. "Leisure" became a pursuit in and of itself, defined as "anything not happening at work." And soon it became monetized, transformed into a market like anything else. The pastimes that once arose from the natural rhythms of community—like festivals and shared meals—were now replaced with organized entertainment, which came with a price tag. Railway companies started offering ticketed events for factory workers, inviting them to escape their labor for a fee. Paid admission to sporting events and other amusements became a way to capitalize on what was once the birthright of every human being: rest and enjoyment.[20]

Leisure was once woven into the fabric of life. It was as natural as breathing, a rhythm that ebbed and flowed with the demands of the day, the needs of the body, the cycles of the earth. Festivals marked the passing of time, and a nap in the afternoon wasn't a luxury but a part of life. Meals were slow, communal, unhurried. There was no line between work and life because life wasn't something to be balanced against work—it simply was. The everyday peasant may not have been rich in material wealth, but they were rich in time, in the unstructured moments that make a life full.

They lived in a tempo that capitalism would soon steal, replacing it with the hurried, commodified version of leisure we know today.[21]

———

I feel the ache of the system we are bound to whenever I try to rush my family out the door in the morning. My kids take their time sliding on their shoes, slow, steady, untouched by the burden of hurry. And there I am, breaking into that beauty with my own impatience, tugging them into a world that runs on deadlines and demands. I find myself whispering "I'm sorry Mama was in a rush today" more than I care to admit, as if I can somehow unteach them the urgency that's bound me all my life.

I want to "unlearn hurrying," as Robin Wall Kimmerer says.[22] I want to stop treating time like it's something slipping away and instead let it hold me. Freedom is learning how to dwell in the slowness, to breathe without the weight of scarcity pressing on my chest. I want that for my kids—to know a life unchained, where they can take their time without the world clawing at their heels.

The question we're left with now is this: How do we reclaim the sacredness of rest in a world that's forgotten how to be still?

Time as Liberator

Decolonizing my relationship to productivity—and in essence to time—began long before our family left the city for a farmhouse in the woods of middle Tennessee. It was the desire to connect to the rhythms of the earth that encouraged us to uproot our lives and begin an endeavor that felt so foreign to me. I knew that tending to the land, caring for animals, and managing our home, children, and writing would demand much from us. Yet I longed to know the earth and her creatures as intimately as I know my own soul.

I didn't anticipate how profoundly the earth's steady cycles would reorient my sense of time, transforming my minutes, hours, days, weeks, months, seasons, and years again and again. Learning to truly live within cyclical time reshaped my sense of productivity. When I am guided by the earth, it is she who dictates when to work and when to rest, freeing me from the need to force productivity into unnatural rhythms.

We often think of time as linear and fixed, moving only in one direction, from past to present to future. Once a moment passes, it's lost forever. But this idea of linear time didn't appear out of nowhere. It emerged during the era of empire building to maximize investments and productivity.

The creation of Greenwich Mean Time in 1884 made time a tool of empire, centering colonial Britain as the world's timekeeper. This imposed standard didn't just regulate time; it also reinforced Western dominance.[23] Cultures with different concepts of time, productivity, and leisure were labeled lazy or primitive, judged by standards that didn't account for their own ways of being. Even today, Western values of punctuality and efficiency are used to dismiss other cultures.[24]

As scholar Walter Mignolo points out, when Europeans classified non-European people first as "barbarian," then as "primitive," it was a classification rooted in time.[25] They were seen as living in the past. This mindset devalued the past as less advanced and less legitimate, and placed Europe in the present as the most advanced civilization.

Colonialism taught that only the Western present was valuable and rejected the past as a source of wisdom.[26] This way of thinking not only downplays the ongoing harm of historical injustices but also promotes the myth of progress, the belief that societies naturally evolve from underdeveloped to developed.

But the earth doesn't follow a linear path. She moves in cycles of growth and decay, rest and renewal. Life is not about constant motion or endless output. It's about knowing when to pause, when to let go, and when to begin again. And maybe that's what decolonizing time looks like—freeing ourselves from the rush, the race, and learning to live in rhythm with the sacred cycles that have always been there, waiting for us to remember. We are linked to both the past and the present, belonging to a lineage that viewed time as a guide, a teacher, a friend, something that helps us become who we are.

John O'Donohue once said that if we see time as the essence of presence, we begin to understand that in the spiritual world "time behaves differently."[27] Consider this verse from Scripture, "With the Lord a single day is like a thousand years and a thousand years are like a single day" (2 Pet. 3:8). Time stretches and folds in on itself, offering a reminder that the divine has a rhythm all its own.

A Holy Pause

> Come to me, all you who are struggling hard and carrying heavy loads, and I will give you rest. Put on my yoke, and learn from me. I'm gentle and humble. And you will find rest for yourselves. My yoke is easy to bear, and my burden is light.
>
> —Matt. 11:28–30

For a long time I believed that this passage referred to "soul weariness," a restlessness that Jesus promises to relieve.[28] And while that's true, I've come to believe that Jesus's words also hold a tangible, material promise. He lived in a world where the poor were relentlessly exploited, a reality that deeply concerned him. Throughout his ministry, Jesus spoke often about the poor and the rich, addressing the injustices of his time. Many of those who followed him were on the lowest economic rung, familiar with burdens. They came to Jesus for both spiritual and physical comfort, seeking relief from harsh realities.

When Jesus invites the weary to come to him for rest, he's offering more than spiritual solace; he's also addressing the oppressive demands placed on their lives. By using the analogy of a yoke—a wooden frame that joins animals together to pull a load—Jesus is making a profound statement. He isn't like the harsh leaders of the world who impose heavy burdens on their subjects through land dispossession, high-interest loans, strict religious requirements, and market manipulation. Instead, Jesus offers a yoke that is easy and a burden that is light, promising true belonging to a kin-dom marked by gentleness, humility, and shared community. A kin-dom where the poor are free from the constant demands of empire. Jesus's message is as much about rest from physical and societal toil as it is about spiritual peace.

Jesus modeled rest in his own life. He took naps in boats in the middle of storms, as if to say there is no urgency great enough to rob us of our rest (Mark 4:38). Before feeding the five thousand, he encouraged his disciples to retreat, to step away from the crowds and find a secluded place to rest (6:31). There's a tenderness in this, a recognition that rest is not a luxury but a holy thing.

This is important because we often see rest as a tool to help us be more efficient later or as a way to prevent burnout, as if burnout is the natural order of things. But here's a truth I find pressing for our time: Never did Jesus say "rest now so you can work harder later." Rest was never framed as something we do only to be more productive afterward. In a world obsessed with efficiency, where rest is seen as a way to recharge for more labor, Jesus shows us something else. He offers rest as an end in itself, as a way of being, a gift that is not earned but given freely. His rest is not about being more useful tomorrow; it's about being fully human today.

As Julia Watts Belser notes, ableism turns simple pleasures like sleeping in or daydreaming into a waste of time, convincing us that slow bodies need fixing. Wandering minds are deemed unacceptable; our thinking must show rigor, seriousness. A slow morning or an afternoon on the couch can be perceived as a moral failing, a sign of weakness rather than a sacred act of care.[29]

In the Genesis creation story, when God separates the light from the darkness on the first day, it isn't morning that comes first but night. This detail is significant. In Jewish tradition, Sabbath starts at sundown. This rhythm reminds us that our days should begin not with work but with rest. This sacred orientation of time itself tells us that our worth is not tied to our labor or our output. Rest is not a reward for hard work, it is a right. This speaks to the fact that creation itself is good, just as it is. She will take care of us.

Rest, then, is an act of trust. Trusting that we don't have to earn our place here. Trusting that we are enough, even when we are still.

Reclaiming the Sacredness of the Body

Christian theology holds the incarnation of Jesus as its heartbeat, the divine embodied. Yet many today shy away from the idea of God having a body. It's curious, really, because Christianity itself is so deeply concerned with the body. Every tradition, every denomination is shaped by it—the body of Christ, the suffering body, the glorified body.

Our faith is undeniably rooted in flesh.

While some imagine God as beyond form, beyond the limits of our physical world, ancient Jewish texts boldly speak of God's face, God's hands. Even if we think of these as metaphors, they point to a mystery: that God transcends our words, our limited understanding. And yet, we are inescapably bodies, living in a world where bodies are so often the site of violence. A world that deems certain bodies—Black, fat, queer, trans, disabled—as unworthy or incompatible with the sacred. This is why theology cannot be separate from the political. It must ask who has been given the power to decide which bodies bear the image of God and how systems of violence use religious language to justify oppression.

Paul's teaching that we are one body with many parts, where the parts we *think* are the weakest are actually the most essential (1 Cor. 12:12–27), is crucial here. He challenges the idea that some members are inherently weaker. Instead, he emphasizes that those we *perceive* as weaker deserve greater honor. This perspective shifts how we value others. We are encouraged to see the importance of

125

every individual as a vital part of the whole and to act with mutual concern and care within the collective.

The hand moves to feed the mouth, to guide a chair, to brush the teeth, one part tending to another. Our relationships—with God, with each other, with the world—are not separate from the whole. But here's the paradox: The whole cannot exist without the self. How we treat our own body matters. It shapes how we love, how we care, how we relate to the bodies around us. "Consider all the times you have assessed your value or lack thereof by comparing yourself to someone else," says Sonya Renee Taylor.[30] When we carry the weight of body shame, we begin to see other bodies as something to envy or judge.

In a society that privileges certain bodies over others, violence is not only in what is done but in what is neglected. Some are lifted high while others are left to wither, unseen. But this kind of violence and dehumanization is not just out there, in the systems and institutions. It thrives in us. We despise others because we despise ourselves, and the reverse is just as true. Even those who wield power with an iron hand are revealing something of how they treat their own selves.[31]

Taylor calls this "hierarchy of bodies" an illusion—a social and colonial construct that fuels power and oppression. We internalize this hierarchy, learning to see our value through its lens.[32] Those who fit the dominant categories sit at the top, not because they are better, but because the world has named them so. And the rest of us? We scramble for footing on the rungs below. We spend our lives trying to climb higher, hoping for power or acceptance, but our ascent comes at the expense of others. Every step up reinforces the very hierarchy that keeps certain bodies beneath us.

None of us are untouched by this. The hierarchy seduces us into dominating not just others but ourselves. We silence and ignore our bodies. We discipline them into submission. We treat our bodies like machines to be manipulated and optimized. The media plays its part in this, stoking our body hatred, feeding the capitalism that thrives on our dissatisfaction. As Jia Tolentino points out in *Trick Mirror*, this is especially true for women. The beauty ideals we're sold do not seek our flourishing. They teach us to shrink, to sculpt ourselves into something palatable. Tolentino names the trouble at the root of this: Mainstream feminism has, at times, had to conform to patriarchy and capitalism just to survive.[33]

If we are to reckon with our complicity in oppressive systems, we must turn inward and examine the quiet, unspoken ways we have learned to shrink, to resent, to war against our own flesh. The undoing begins here, within the bodies we have been taught to distrust. Injustice endures not just because of laws and policies but because we have not yet made peace with the bodies we live in—our own or one another's. Decolonizing, then, is about tending to what has been colonized within us. This is not just about individual transformation but also a commitment to fostering collective change. We cannot build something in the world that we haven't first cultivated within ourselves.[34] And doing so requires a love that is neither sentimental nor passive, but radical. A love that restores dignity where it has been eroded, that names what has been lost and refuses to lose it again. Those who have learned this love, who know their worth, who have wrestled with shame and come out still standing are often the ones able to challenge the world's hierarchies. They organize, they create, they tell stories that bear witness. Their very existence, unashamed and unbowed, becomes a form of resistance.

Prayer of Resistance

Divine Rest,

We are weary and bent, our bodies burdened by the weight of empire's demands. Forgive us, for some of us have worshiped the hustle, others of us have fallen for the lie that our value is measured in labor. We confess that in our striving we've silenced the unique song of our bodies, treating rest as weakness and the divine worth of all flesh as lesser. But hear us now, in stillness, as we reclaim our worth.

We breathe in mercy, and with every exhale we return to the sacredness of rest.

Benediction

May we remember that our bodies are sacred vessels—carrying life, love, spirit. We were crafted not for profit but for purpose, woven with intention. We are not commodities; we are beloved, whole, and free.

Let us rest in the truth that we are sacred, and we are enough.
Amen.

CHAPTER 7

Rejecting Sameness, Embracing Wholeness

Invocation

Divine Diversity, root us in rememberance. Help us honor where we come from, resist the forces that erase our sacred particularity, and delight in the beauty of what makes us unique.

We honor who we are. We reject that which seeks to divide and diminish us.

Reflection

The people of West Africa tell a story about a tortoise who refused to assimilate:

> *Long ago in the forests of West Africa, the animals lived in harmony with the land. Among them was a clever tortoise named Adanko. One day a group of foreign animals arrived, bringing new ways and strange customs. They demanded that the animals of the forest abandon their traditions and adopt theirs, which they claimed were superior. Most*

animals, fearing conflict, complied. The birds stopped singing their ancestral songs, the monkeys gave up their playful games, and even the mighty elephant began to follow the foreign ways. But Adanko refused.

"Why should we forget who we are?" he asked. "Our ways have sustained us for generations." The foreign animals scoffed at him.

"You are just a slow, small tortoise. What do you know about power?"

Adanko smiled. "Power is not in speed or size. It lies in knowing oneself."

Determined to prove him wrong, the foreigners challenged Adanko to a race, believing their faster animals would easily win. But Adanko, wise and patient, took his time. While the others hurried and exhausted themselves, Adanko stayed steady, following his own path. By sunset, Adanko had reached the finish, while the others lay scattered and weary. The forest animals, seeing the tortoise's victory, remembered their own strength and returned to their traditions, rejecting the foreign ways that had made them forget their roots.

Those who have ears let them hear.

On Monday, March 27, 2023, a gunman stormed through a K–6 grade school in Nashville, killing six people, three of them nine-year-old children. The tragedy unfolded only miles from where I sat with my family that day, but its weight stretched far outside the city. It became Tennessee's deadliest mass shooting, sending shockwaves across the state and beyond. In the aftermath, hundreds of demonstrators gathered at the state capitol, calling for an end to the madness. Among them were Reps.

Gloria Johnson, Justin Jones, and Justin Pearson, standing with those who cried out for stricter gun laws.

But instead of being heard, the representatives were accused of disorder; their peaceful protest was even likened to the violence of the January 6th insurrection. And in a move that bore the weight of history, the Tennessee House voted to expel Jones and Pearson, both young Black men, while Johnson, a white woman, narrowly escaped the same fate. When asked why she wasn't expelled, Johnson didn't mince words: "I think it's pretty clear. I'm a sixty-year-old white woman, and they are two young Black men."[1] Her voice trembled with the truth of it—how deeply race shapes who is seen, who is silenced, who is allowed to challenge power, and who is seen as worthy of being in the room.

Johnson explained that the attitude of the House was, "You have to assimilate into this body to be one of us. If you're going to come into this body, you have to act like this body." In other words, "You can't dress like that on the floor."[2] Earlier that year, Rep. Pearson had drawn scrutiny for wearing a dashiki—traditional West African attire and a symbol of his heritage—during his swearing-in ceremony. After his clothing was criticized by another member, Pearson took to X (formerly Twitter) to denounce the remarks. The Tennessee House GOP responded, telling Pearson that if he didn't like the rules, he should "explore a different career opportunity."[3] But what they were really saying was that belonging comes at the cost of conformity. You can be here only if you make yourself quieter, smaller. But Pearson had refused to lay down the fullness of who he was just to fit into the rules of power. And in his defiance, there is a hope that the walls of this House might one day look different, sound different, be different.

Belonging Across Boundaries

Empires demand conformity as a means of control. To belong, you have to look, act, and ultimately reflect the empire itself.

This creates a false sense of unity while stripping away what makes us different. Yet the irony lies in the fact that empires have also relied on a variety of ethnicities, cultures, and religions for their survival—although this diversity has never been one of equality. Empire benefits the powerful while forcing the rest to conform.

Look at the Roman Empire, vast and full of difference, but only on the surface. Beneath, Rome was crafting an illusion of cohesion, pressuring people to erase their languages, their faiths, their ethnic and cultural ways of being. This "unity" was created to achieve control. The Greeks knew how to do this too. Alexander the Great's project of Hellenization sought to make the ancient world look, sound, and think Greek. It became the thread that tied people together, but as subjects rather than as equals.[4] In the world of empire, belonging has always been conditional. To belong is to assimilate, and to assimilate is to surrender who you are.

———

From the beginning of his political career, Donald Trump has used racist tropes to position himself as the protector of America's declining white majority—a common rhetoric of emperors across history. His campaigns have been filled with promises to "Make America Great Again" by building a "big, beautiful wall" along the US-Mexican border and demonizing Latin American countries. Like many rulers before him, Trump crafted a narrative that portrayed the "other" as criminal invaders, regardless of age, gender, or their reason for migration.

I made my first trip to Trump's wall along the US-Mexico border in 2018 as part of *las posadas*, a ritual performed in many Latin American countries and immigrant communities in the United States. It reenacts and commemorates Mary and Joseph's pilgrimage to Bethlehem and their search for a place to belong. Typically, *las posadas* last nine days and are performed just before Christmas.

But on this day, we walked miles in remembrance and solidarity with our siblings on the other side of the border.

Our journey began with a two-mile trek through the desert, which eventually opened onto an untouched stretch of beach. In the distance, the border fence loomed, cutting across the sand and disappearing into the Pacific Ocean. Border patrol officers stood like sentinels along the fence, armed with guns and wearing helmets and vests. As we approached the fence, they led us to a space they called Friendship Park. The irony was thick in the air. This park was meant to be a place where families on both sides of the border could meet and embrace; now it felt like a monument to the separation. Instead of fresh lawn and inviting picnic benches, there is a swath of churned-up earth telling a story of what could've been.

Our time was marked by Christmas hymns across the wall and the calling out of *presente*, which is a way of honoring those who died crossing the border that year by saying their names aloud. As each name was read, I thought of my own family, the desperation that had pushed them to leave everything behind. Every name felt personal—like a prayer whispered for my own mother and grandfather, tia and tio.

Though the wall blocked our view, we heard our Mexican neighbors rising up in song on the other side. Our voices met theirs, defying the cold steel between us. It was a moment of unshakable solidarity against the boundaries that tried to keep us apart. We ended with celebration, a declaration that music and sounds, like presence, can transcend any barrier.

I couldn't see the Tijuana side of the wall, but I knew it was far from cold and lifeless. Over there, life buzzes with people selling goods, mariachis singing love songs, children playing. The wall on the Tijuana side is alive with colorful graffiti full of messages—both sentimental and political. But on the American side? Men in uniform, trucks, helicopters, guns, and the cold gray steel of division.

Reflecting on this contrast, Luis Alberto Urrea once posed a poignant question: Who truly is free and who is the prisoner?[5] Standing there, with the image so clear, I wondered the same thing.

———

Colonialism has left its deep marks on this world, reshaping landscapes, uprooting peoples, and reordering systems in ways that echo through time. Perhaps one of the most profound legacies was the mass migration and forced settlement of Europeans across the Americas, Africa, and beyond—a movement that altered the very makeup of global populations. British and French legal systems laid the foundations of governance, crafting the economies and political powers we live under today. The transformation of empires into nation-states fundamentally redefined how we understand belonging and power.

The idea of the nation-state, born in European thought in the seventeenth and eighteenth centuries, wasn't about sovereign rulers anymore; it was about people. A nation-state is imagined as a place where those within its borders share a common language, culture, or religion. But let's be clear: No nation has ever fully realized that ideal. So nation-states had to be built, deliberately constructed with lines and borders that were more than geographic; they marked out who was worthy of protection and inclusion. This is the paradox of the nation: It holds out the promise of belonging, but only for those who fit the mold. Everyone else? They are kept at bay.

Borders give governments the power to function, to tax, to police, and to control. Porous borders make it difficult to control a population. A fixed one makes it easier. Colonial powers carved out borders to organize the world in ways that worked to their own advantage. The lines we now see dividing countries and cultures, peoples and languages, minds and ways of knowing were drawn with the tools of empire. The idea was simple but dangerous, that a nation should consist of people who are alike in every way. Those who looked, spoke, or worshiped differently were a threat to the "imagined community" of the nation. Benedict Anderson uses the phrase "imagined community" to describe how the United States and other nations constructed their identities.[6] The community is imagined because the people within a nation share a sense of common history and values, even when that story is woven from myths and selective memory. Through shared symbols and stories they feel are uniquely "theirs," the people develop a sense of camaraderie. They believe they know each other, but in reality, they don't. And this imagined community has the power to stir up a sense of belonging that people will fight for, even die for. That's the allure, and the danger, of nationalism. It tells you that you're a part of something but often only by turning you against someone else. It is argued that this nationalist way of thinking is something we inherited from colonizers. Even our imaginations remain colonized.

The nation-state, in all its abstraction, has become the canvas onto which we project ideals about race, religion, language, culture, and history. Over time this sense of national identity binds itself to culture in a way that fosters an us-versus-them mentality. We see this clearly in the United States, where national identity is often constructed by identifying enemies—whether communists in the past or Latin American immigrants today. The threat of the outsider has been a constant tool to unite peoples.

The idea that a nation must be built on a single race, language, or religion has fueled some of history's darkest moments, from Nazi Germany to modern expressions of white supremacy and Christian nationalism. Trumpism has reignited these fears back into the heart of national identity, reminding us that the borders we draw in the world often start in our minds.

The work of healing from colonialism begins when we stop seeing ourselves as separate from others, when we stop imagining the border as a line to defend and instead recognize it as a wound in need of healing.

Confronting the Theology of Manifest Destiny

The United States' rise to superpower status has been driven by violent military campaigns and economic exploitation. From devastating wars in Asia and the Middle East that claimed countless innocent lives to financial control over Latin America, this nation's story is one of dominance.

Beneath this pursuit of power lies a belief in its divine mission, rooted in the conviction that Americans are a chosen people. From its founding, Manifest Destiny framed US expansion as a divine mission to spread superior governance and redeem other nations. The Puritans saw America as a new promised land, binding national growth to the spread of Christianity—intertwining religious identity with imperial ambition.

This vision of the United States as a "new Israel" fueled the belief in American exceptionalism—the idea that America is divinely chosen to be a beacon to the world, or a "city on a hill," as John Winthrop declared to his fellow Puritans.[7] The Pilgrims and Puritans, fleeing religious persecution in England, equated their culture with divine purpose. This fostered what Kelly Brown Douglas calls "the Anglo-Saxon myth," which took root at the heart of American identity, shaping everything from politics to an understanding of democracy and freedom. But the promise of liberty remained selective.[8]

The belief in divine chosenness justified the theft of Native lands, the genocide of Native peoples, forced conversions, and the horrors of slavery—all backed up by a theology that upheld white supremacy.[9] As Willie James Jennings explains, Christian theology became entangled with the racial hierarchies that segregated and subjugated communities, forcing them to adapt and conform to the colonial order."[10] Those who couldn't assimilate—Native, Black, or otherwise—were deemed uncivilized or subhuman. Those who dared to resist were met with violence.[11]

Christian entanglement with the militarized approach of Manifest Destiny is grounded in the image of Christ as a warrior who conquers rather than communes, who subdues rather than restores. But a Christ shaped by the logic of empire cannot be the Christ who washed feet, who wept, who refused the sword. Theologian Catherine Keller urges us to "free the messianic from the imperial imaginary, divine and human." She reminds us that even liberation theologians can fall into the trap of envisioning a "messianic warrior-liberator" who enforces change through violence.[12] It's time to reckon with the way faith has been co-opted to uphold empire, to unweave the threads of imperial ambition from our theology, and to reimagine a Messiah who leads not with domination but with love.

———

It was my second night in Haiti when the sound of drums and chanting jolted me awake. One of my teammates unzipped my tent, "Kat, we're going inside to pray." When I arrived, the group had already formed a circle, murmuring prayers and asking for protection against evil. Outside, a group of local Haitians had gathered, engaging in what seemed like a spiritual ritual directed at our camp. We were certain it was meant to harm us, convinced we were caught in some cosmic battle of good versus evil. And why wouldn't we believe that? It was the story we had been handed about Haiti. The "lostness" and "darkness" of the people there was what justified our mission in the first place.

But I wonder now if their gathering was less about curses and more about protest, a resistance to the quiet audacity of a group of foreigners like us walking their streets, their land, with no real understanding of the history, the injustice, the oppression etched into its soil. We meant well, but our theology was too thin to hold the weight of the harm we carried with us. Perhaps their midnight visit was less of an attack and more of a lament.

137

On a later trip, I saw a group of white missionaries, their bright green T-shirts shouting, "Hope for Haiti." I scoffed, but deep down I knew I was guilty of the same patronizing posture. I came believing I brought the hope they needed. I left with a sense of "gratitude" and "humility." Every debrief circled the same thought: how "they" had so little and yet seemed so content. But even in my good intentions, I was ignorant of my pride.

One afternoon we were sent to walk through neighborhoods and ask if anyone needed prayer. People nodded, weary, asking for prayers for tangible needs. We prayed and offered them Bibles instead. I'll never forget one woman's response, "Thank you, but I already have Bibles. I don't need more; I need glasses to read the ones I have." I felt so useless. What was I even doing there? I don't recall what we did next—probably left the Bible anyway, convinced we'd "been obedient." But I remember I couldn't shake the ache of a faith that didn't seem to see her at all.

That Bible would come to symbolize the disconnect I was grappling with. We handed out Bibles as if they could heal wounds we weren't willing to see while ignoring not only the real, urgent needs of the people but also the systems of exploitation that had brought this suffering upon Haiti in the first place.

I first visited Haiti in December 2013, two decades after a coup overthrew its first democratically elected president, Jean-Bertrand Aristide. A champion of the poor, his voice was too bold for those in power, so they exiled him through force, and the country was thrown into violence and bloodshed. Thousands fled, only to be denied refuge in the United States.

US Marines later arrived and returned Aristide to office, calling it a restoration of democracy. In reality, they protected coup leaders while stripping Aristide of power.[13]

This was just one chapter in a long history of US interference. After Haiti's 1915 presidential assassination, US troops occupied the country, draining its financial reserves, rewriting its constitution, and tethering its economy to American control for decades.

What Americans called order, Haitians experienced as exploitation—a slow siphoning of sovereignty disguised as salvation.

The occupation's brutality was chilling. Marines kicked around decapitated heads to terrorize rebels, publicly executed resistance fighters, and forced Haitians into labor camps that resembled a national chain gang. Over fifteen thousand Haitians were killed, and even after the occupation ended in 1934, US leaders continued meddling in Haitian elections.[14]

These are the scars of a country that dared first to resist. While still under French rule, Haiti became the first independent Black republic in 1804 after the successful Haitian Revolution. But this struck fear in the hearts of slave-owning nations like the United States, which saw Haiti's rebellion as a threat to American slavery. In retaliation, the United States refused to recognize the new nation, isolating it economically and politically. Rejection and exploitation, rooted in fear of Black liberation, haunts the relationship between Haiti and the United States to this day. Consider the way Donald Trump has spoken about Haiti, whether in 2018, when he used vulgar and disparaging language to describe the country, or in 2024, when he spread unfounded rumors about Haitian immigrants. Both instances reinforced harmful stereotypes that have long influenced US perceptions and policies toward the country.

I share this history because it's often missing from the narrative of well-meaning American missionaries, myself included. What "hope" were we really bringing to Haiti? Thousands of us flood the country each year, convinced we are bringing the gospel to people we assume are spiritually impoverished, never pausing to consider how Haitians feel about our presence or to question whether they need what we've come to give. With so many ministries on the island, are Haitian people truly ignorant of the gospel? Are there still those left who have yet to hear the message of Jesus?

I remember a day when we encountered a woman we believed was demon-possessed. She screamed at us in Creole as we handed out Bibles, but instead of trying to understand, we turned to prayer, convinced her cries were the work of darkness. Our translator didn't explain her anger, and we took it as confirmation that we were casting out evil spirits. But now I wonder if she wasn't possessed at all, just as I wonder about the group who came to visit us in the night. Perhaps instead, like the others, she was crying out against the centuries of exploitation her people had endured at the hands of outsiders like we were. Maybe it wasn't she who needed deliverance but us.

Yet we left with triumphant stories of spiritual warfare, tales of how we drove out demons, how our presence was such a threat to demonic powers that the locals came to cast spells on us with drums and chanting.

Edward Said once wrote, "Stories are at the heart of what explorers and novelists say about strange regions of the world."[15] While the real battle of imperialism may be over land, it is through stories that questions of belonging, power, and what the future holds are contested and ultimately decided. Nations and borders are themselves narrations, stories we construct and enforce. Said reminds us that the power to tell or silence certain stories is not just central to culture and imperialism; it is the very link between them.[16] And yet, it is also through stories that the colonized have resisted, reclaiming their identities and histories in the face of domination.

In Haiti, we perpetuated the colonial narrative that salvation required praying like us, thinking like us, becoming like us. We carried the assumption that to truly know God, Haitians had to adopt our ways of worship and theology. In doing so, we were reenacting the legacy of European colonization. The missionary has long been an agent of cultural expansion, shaping the world according to a single story. And in many ways, that remains true today.[17]

I visited Haiti the second time with the megachurch I attended. It had launched its twenty thousand souls saved by 2020 campaign—an effort that included planting churches in other countries. There was no doubt that this church did a lot for Miami, dedicating its resources and connections to serving the largely La-tino congregation and their families in Latin America. By the time I left, they had campuses in the Dominican Republic and Costa Rica. But I kept asking myself, *why?* Why did they feel the need to export their American theologies, their polished ideologies, and their shiny media presentations into these places rather than using their resources to support the churches that were already there?

It's as if the church was carrying forward the same thread of Manifest Destiny, still driven by the belief that it had to go out and conquer new lands, that its version of faith was the one that would save the world. But I wonder, what if instead of bringing salvation we were simply repackaging the same old colonialism wrapped in Scripture?

Words as Empire's Weapons

According to Robert Paul Seesengood, William Carey's 1793 ser-mon "An Inquiry into the Obligation of Christians to Use Means for the Conversion of the Heathens" sparked the modern missions movement. The sermon went "viral" for its time, spread as an eighty-seven-page tract throughout the English-speaking world. Carey's message drew from Paul's missionary journeys and Jesus's command in Acts 1:8 to "be my witnesses in Jerusalem, in all Judea and Samaria, and to the end of the earth." This same verse was plastered on the T-shirts I wore during short-term mission trips, created by the church that sent us out. It was a blueprint for how we were to reach "the world." We were "commissioned": first, to be witnesses in our own city (Jerusalem), then to reach our country (Judea and Samaria), and finally to extend our mission to foreign lands, "the end of the earth."

Carey also argued for the Bible's infallibility, or the belief that it is without error. He taught that evangelism and handing out the Bible as an authoritative text were not just important but "morally obligatory." What followed in the century to come was a massive surge in Bible translations, growing from 50 to 250, and a rise in missionary societies, multiplying into the hundreds.[18]

As Christianity spread worldwide, so did various debates about the nature of Scripture—its infallibility, its inerrancy, and the authority of Paul's letters. These debates undergirded the cultural dominance of colonial Christianity, which went hand in hand with the supremacy of the English language. As the gospel was preached, so too was English imposed, becoming the official language in many colonized regions. Missions became less about spreading the gospel and more about shaping colonized people in the image of the colonizers.[19]

————

There's something sacred in the way words stretch themselves, holding infinite possibilities. The right words can unlock universes. When strung together, they spark something within us.[20] Brené Brown speaks of language as "our portal to meaning-making, connection, healing, learning, and self-awareness." But she also reminds us that "having access" is the key.[21]

We begin our lives without "language" as we know it. In those first years of life, we rely on our bodies to express what words cannot. I think about when my kids were learning to speak. How hard it was for them not to be able to tell me what they needed. They would tense up, groan, stomp their little feet in frustration, their bodies becoming the language they hadn't yet mastered. It was a lesson for me, not just in patience and empathy but in the *limits* of language itself. This has made me more hesitant to romanticize it. We love to talk about words with wonder on our tongues, emphasizing the magic and beauty that language holds. But the truth is that as much as it connects, it also divides. In a global community, language is often *the thing* that keeps us apart.

We can't ignore the link between language and empire. This is because language is never innocent; it's a battleground, where the powerful carve out their dominance and the oppressed struggle to be heard.[22] We see this in the way a "standard" version of language is imposed through education and social structures, and anything outside it treated as an impurity.[23] When we speak, our words are never just about syntax and grammar; they're about embodying the weight of a culture and a civilization.[24] We carry within our words the histories we've inherited and the worlds we envision. In this way, language isn't just a tool for communication but also a way of being, a living reality.[25] It houses our stories, our bodies, our dreams realized and deferred. It's the place where memory and the present meet. This is why language is central to decolonization. In colonized nations, independence has almost always meant reclaiming a language as a way of reclaiming identity.

Haitian Creole is a beautiful example of a language born out of resistance to colonization. Budding from the cracks of French rule, Haitian Creole—a blend of African languages with French—was once dismissed as an inferior dialect; today, it testifies to the resilience and creativity of the oppressed.[26]

Even Spanish, the tongue of my people, exists in a similar liminal space. It was the language of conquerors, used to silence Indigenous voices. But here in the United States, it's a language of the marginalized, often dismissed and treated as inferior. My abuela lived here for more than half her life and never did learn to speak English. "¡En español!" she'd insist whenever conversations drifted away from her mother tongue. I see it as her quiet rebellion, her defiance against empire's reach, as if to say, my voice will not bend to your tongue.

Though there's beauty in Spanish, I recognize its violent history. Spanish is not the original language of my ancestors. Language, never innocent, always re-creates. But it's not Spanish that liberates me; it is the hybrid, the half-breath, the improvised word that sets me free. In the same way that Creole is a blend of languages, *Spanglish* is a mixture of Spanish and English. It's a way of thinking and being that lives beyond borders. It moves and stretches between worlds and cultures, revealing lives that don't exist neatly within the confines of any one identity.

No wonder I felt drawn to Creole when I lived in New Orleans. Something about the blend of languages in the in-between spaces spoke to a part of my spirit in ways I still struggle to articulate. Perhaps that's because language isn't a thin window to communication. It is dense, weighted with meaning, memory, and place—as real and rooted as the body.

In the spaces where languages collide and coalesce, something deeper is happening. It's in these hybrid places where I feel most at home, where I catch glimpses of a life beyond empire's grasp. Here, language—imperfect yet alive—becomes more than just a tool. It becomes a space where freedom stirs and takes root beyond the borders and limits of a single story.

Reclaiming Language from Babel to Pentecost

In Genesis 11, we find the story of Babel. A story of a people united under a single language, their voices and words one. They gather at Shinar with a desire to build a tower with its top in the sky, to craft a name for themselves so strong it'll hold them together (v. 4). They begin building, stone upon stone, but then God descends, watches, and feels the weight of their uniformity. In a breath, God chooses to disrupt their language, splintering their words, scattering them across the earth.

I was told that this story is about human arrogance—people trying to touch the heavens. And maybe that's part of it. But looking closer now, I see something more. I see a people seeking to consolidate power. They weren't just building a tower to get to God; they were building an empire so they could act as one. "Let's make a name for ourselves," they said, and that name was to be unmatched. Their desire was to become a civilization that would dominate others.[27] They craved homogeneity, a single language, a monoculture. An identity that would be untouchable, universal, pure. But their tower rose only through the labor of others, laid brick by brick on the backs of those beneath them.[28]

But God intervenes, not to punish them, but to disrupt their project of homogenization. God creates diversity where there was uniformity, scattering them with new languages, new cultures, and a plethora of voices. They wanted control, but God imposed chaos— a kind of holy chaos that prevents the concentration of power.

Walter Brueggemann speaks to this, noting that a human unity, when built outside God's will, often ends in "oppressive conformity."[29] The people of Babel weren't just unified; they were uniform. And in that uniformity was a desire to control what was different and unpredictable. But the Spirit of God is a Spirit of disruption, making space for the multitude of stories that refuse to stay silent.

This, after all, is what we see at Pentecost. Acts 2 says that a sound like rushing wind filled the room and a flame rested on each person that was gathered. Suddenly, they began speaking in other tongues. Jews from every nation were in Jerusalem to celebrate the Feast of Pentecost; hearing the commotion, they drew near. And to their wonder, each one heard their own native language. "Aren't all these people Galileans?" they asked. Yet every word came alive in their hearts, as if spoken just for them. Bewildered, they wondered, "What does this mean?"

This scene at Pentecost is almost too wild to imagine. Wind, fire, voices rising in a cacophony. It's chaos, and it is precisely this chaos that reveals something holy. At that moment, the Roman Empire ruled over Jerusalem, a land where displaced Jewish people from every corner of the diaspora gathered. They came speaking different languages, shaped by different sects and stories, their lives marked by the weight of constant displacement. And yet, in this scene, they are all together, bound by their shared longing for something more.

In the midst of this, Jesus's followers are waiting. They have been promised something, something from the same God who has a way of showing up in unexpected places. And on that day of Pentecost, God arrives once again, not in predictability but in a breath of fire and confusion, much like at Babel. The Spirit falls like a storm, poured out on all people just as the prophet Joel had declared. And the thing that strikes me most about this scene isn't that God shows up but how the Spirit's arrival is wrapped in chaos—a stunning contrast to the order and control that empires crave.

At that time, Latin was the official tongue of Rome, but Greek was the common language most understood. So when those gathered around the apostles heard the native languages of their scattered homes being spoken by Galileans, they were mystified. "How can this be?" they asked. The Spirit allowing each person to hear in their own language wasn't just a miracle; it was a direct challenge to the imperial order. It was as if God was saying, *You will not erase the tongues of my people.*

The divine Spirit doesn't arrive in the tidy ways empire wants, with its thirst for predictability and properness. No, the Spirit comes in the chaos that leaves us wide-eyed, amazed, and mystified. I love that the crowd's first response was astonishment, confusion. That's what happens when the Spirit moves. Everything we thought we knew—our understanding of the world, our expectations, our control—is broken open. And in that breaking, something wild and beautiful is born.

It wasn't just the fire or the wind that left the people in awe but the familiar sound of their own languages echoing through the heart of an empire that had long sought to strip them of such things. The same empire that demanded their silence, that told its subjects to abandon their native tongues, now found itself undone by a God using language not to dominate but to liberate. Too many have wielded language as a weapon, forcing those they subjugate to conform to their way of speaking, of being. Christianity, bound up as it has been with empire, has too often been complicit in this, insisting that to belong one must speak the language of power, must fit the mold of the dominant culture.

But in Acts 2, the Spirit moves to unmake this story. The Spirit of God does not ask us to contort ourselves into something we are not. There is no demand for assimilation, no hierarchy of languages or cultures. No single race, class, or status holds dominance in the kin-dom of God. Instead, the Spirit invites us to be the fullest expression of who we are, in all our particularity, in all our strangeness and beauty.

Empire—whether Roman, American, or Christian—will not have the final word. The Spirit of God subverts its logic, calling forth the richness of every tongue, every story, every people. The multitude of voices will always rise, because this is how God works. God is in the midst of the holy chaos, in the languages and people that empire could never quite silence.

Prayer of Resistance

Sacred Multitude,

We hear you in every language, every dialect, every sound that stirs the heart and shakes the earth. At Babel, you shattered the walls of a singular tongue, and in that shattering we found our freedom. We confess the times we've sought comfort in sameness, when we've turned away from the beauty of difference. We embrace your mercy so that we may walk in wholeness.

Open our ears to the voices we have ignored, open our hearts to the beauty we have feared.

Benediction

May our traditions breathe in the spaces we inhabit, a living testament to all that our ancestors dreamed and endured. May we walk with courage, embracing the richness of every voice and the radiance of difference. May we know we are held in a love that has no borders, a love that calls us into the fullness of who we were meant to be.

Amen.

CHAPTER 8

Rejecting Dominance, Embracing Connection

Invocation

Presence Who Holds Sky and Sea, in the breath of the wind and the pull of the tides, remind us that we belong to one another—creatures of soil and spirit, woven into the sacred web of earth.
We acknowledge our place in the balance of life.

Reflection

The Aboriginal people of Australia tell a story about a greedy frog:

Long ago, in the heart of the Australian outback, there lived a greedy frog named Tiddalik. One day, overcome by an unquenchable thirst, he drank all the water in the land—every river, creek, and billabong—leaving the earth dry and cracked. Without water, the other animals grew desperate. The trees wilted, the birds' songs fell silent, and the kangaroos' powerful legs weakened. The animals gathered to devise a plan. They knew Tiddalik wouldn't release the water unless they made him laugh. But how to make such a grumpy frog laugh? One by one, the animals tried. The emu danced a silly jig, the kookaburra cackled his loudest laugh, and the wombat rolled down a hill, but Tiddalik remained stone-faced.

Finally, Nabunum the eel slithered forward and twisted himself into such strange, contorted shapes that even the serious Tiddalik couldn't resist. His belly shook, and a deep rumble of laughter burst from him. As he laughed, the water gushed from his mouth, flooding the land once more. The rivers flowed again, the trees drank deeply, and life returned to the land. The animals rejoiced, grateful for the water, and Tiddalik learned that holding too much for oneself only brings misery.

Those who have ears let them hear.

My home sits tucked away off a gravel road in the foothills of middle Tennessee where the woods creep up to meet us. We bought this land—five acres, they say, of property that is ours—but deep down we know this land doesn't belong to us, not really. It stretches beyond what our feet have touched, up the forested hills, far into the trees. Our legal name might be on it, but in my bones I know it's not ours to claim. We are visitors here. This place belongs to the shrews and cicadas, the wild turkeys and woodpeckers, the bullfrogs and box turtles, the bucks that wander and the heron that graces us with her presence down by the pond now and again.

Before us, this land was home to the Tsalaguwetiyi, the Eastern Band of the Cherokee. Before them, it was believed to be the land of the Yuchi. These peoples lived in communion with this earth, with the rivers and forests that nurtured them. Every year they came together for the Green Corn Ceremony, which was more than a harvest festival; it was a sacred gathering. The Yuchi understood that the earth gives life, and they offered their gratitude in return. For days, they would fast and sing, dance and pray, all to honor the land that sustained them, to restore harmony between themselves and the earth.

I think about the Green Corn Ceremony at the end of every summer when the air shifts and the earth feels heavy with memory. I imagine what it must have been like, the sound of feet dancing on soil, voices lifted in reverence. And so I walk into the woods, down to the creek that flows quietly behind our house. I stand there, still, and listen for the earth's stories—stories of struggle and resistance, of survival and growth. I hear the echoes of a time when people knew that the land is sacred, not to be owned but to be cared for. And in that moment, I remember that we are part of something so much larger than ourselves, something ancient and alive. The earth holds our histories, and if we listen closely, she'll tell them to us again.

———

In 2008, Ecuador became the first country in the world to recognize the rights of nature in its constitution. Imagine that—granting nature the same rights as human beings, to exist, to thrive, and to regenerate. This represented a profound shift in how we could see the world. Instead of treating nature as property to be owned and exploited, Ecuador recognized ecosystems as living entities with inherent value. The change came after strong advocacy by Indigenous communities and environmental organizations, who knew that land is not a resource to be used up but a living being with whom we are in relationship.

This belief was put to the test in 2011, when people in Loja Province sued Ecuador's government for dumping waste into the Vilcabamba River. And they won. The river was given the right to flourish. Indigenous groups followed suit, protecting other sacred rivers like the Piatúa and ecosystems like the Rio Blanco and Los Cedros Cloud Forest from destructive projects.

Ecuador, one of the most biodiverse countries in the world, has become a global leader in recognizing nature's rights—despite its postcolonial reality and the pressures of deforestation and mining. It offers us a reminder that the land has its own voice, one we must learn to listen to and defend. In the face of empire and exploitation, Ecuador has chosen to honor that voice. For them, it is an ancient wisdom that has pulsed for centuries. A wisdom the world is only now beginning to name.

The Quechua call it *sumak kawsay*, which means *buen vivir* or "good living," a philosophy and way of being where the fullness of one life cannot be severed from the flourishing of the whole. It didn't begin as a law or policy but as a rhythm and a knowing. It is a people's song woven into soil and sky, whispering that to live well is to live in balance—with self, with neighbor, with earth.[1]

Jesus, too, spoke of such a life: "The thief enters only to steal, kill, and destroy. I came so that they could have life—indeed, so that they could live life to the fullest" (John 10:10). Empire is the thief, its hands dripping with the blood of the innocent, its feet standing on stolen land. But *sumak kawsay* resists. It measures abundance not through accumulation but by the flourishing of human and nonhuman alike. The fullness of life comes through harmony, reciprocity, and care.

This is nature's own ethos, organisms functioning with a shared intention to sustain life. As Azita Ardakani Walton observes, ecosystems aren't ruled by self-interest or rigid structures. If something no longer contributes to the vitality of the whole, nature shifts, adapts, and changes direction. But humanity resists change. Instead, it fixates on strategies and systems that keep us tethered to ways of being that harm ourselves and the earth.[2] *Sumak kawsay* calls us back, urging us to loosen our grip and live as nature does—fluid, adaptive, attuned to the sacred web of life.

We were made for a world where all beings are worthy of attention and protection: a world where prosperity equates to holy harmony, faith is found in reciprocity, and love is shown through communal care.

Propaganda Etched in Stone

Empire has always sought to extend its reach beyond human dominion, staking its claim on creation itself. Rome, in particular, proclaimed its authority over the very fabric of the cosmos—bending rivers to its will, carving roads through mountains, and imposing order on untamed landscapes. The Empire's ambition left scars, not unlike those we see today in polluted waters, scorched earth, and air thick with waste.[3] But Rome didn't lament this destruction—it celebrated it as victory.

In victory processions, Rome paraded its spoils through the streets: statues from conquered nations, enslaved captives, and treasures stripped from the earth. As scholar Barbara Rossing notes, Rome's ambition extended to the whole *oikoumenē*—the inhabited world—what they called "the end of the earth."[4] This phrase, "the end of the earth," is one that Luke subverts in Acts 1:8. He repurposes the language of empire to describe the spread of Jesus's kin-dom, one built not on domination but on the expansive love of God. The irony is that this verse was co-opted by colonial missionaries to justify their conquests. Scripture, in this way, is a tool of both liberation and oppression, and we must hold the tension, recognizing how it has been wielded for harm and for healing.

The Romans knew the art of domination and carved it into stone. On their statues and coins, emperors gripped the world in their hands, standing triumphantly above it. Some coins told a crueler story, portraying conquered peoples as bound figures—feminized, passive, and helpless.[5] There was intention in this. Rome saw conquest as a kind of emasculation, the subjugated lands made "female" in their defeat, submitting to a power they could never match.[6]

In the city of Aphrodisias, sculptures immortalized Roman emperors, cast as victors over lands personified as women, their power towering above limp and defeated bodies. Claudius is there, dragging Britannia by her hair, his knee pressed to her spine, violence poised and ready. Nero clutches Armenia, her body sagging in defeat.[7] Then there's Trajan's Column in Rome, what's been called "a kind of Tower of Babel," a vision of an eternal empire.[8] Chronicling Rome's conquest of Romania in the Dacian Wars, the scenes carved into the rock tell stories of imperial conquest: forests razed, rivers assaulted, resources extracted. All of it underscored by the empire's gendered violence.[9]

Historian Susan Cole argues that the key to instilling social values is eroticizing them.[10] Jia Tolentino echoes this: "We can decode social priorities through looking at what's most commonly eroticized: male power and female submission, male violence and female pain."[11] For this reason, we need a philosophy to guide us that recognizes that the earth's suffering is tied up in the suffering of the vulnerable—women, the poor, the colonized. To heal one, we must be willing to confront and heal them all.

Liberating Women and Nature

In 1974, the French feminist Françoise d'Eaubonne gifted us the term *ecofeminism*.[12] With it, she expressed something that had long been true: The same structures that exploit the earth also oppress women. Her vision of liberation recognized that the flourishing of one was bound up in the flourishing of the other.[13] D'Eaubonne saw patriarchy's fingerprints all over the environmental crises and the systemic subjugation of women urging a revolution led by those who had suffered most under its weight.

In ancient societies, many cultures honored female deities as creators and protectors.[14] Pachamama, the Incan Mother Earth, was revered as the source of life, overseeing the harvests and ensuring the land's fertility.[15] Yet with the arrival of European colonizers and their patriarchal systems, such deities were silenced. After the Spanish conquered the Americas, Pachamama was replaced by the Virgin Mary, reflecting a shift in power that supressed the sacred feminine and reinforced the submission of women.[16] Where they had once been seen as protectors, women became subjects in a new order that placed men—and male gods—at the top.

As war, violence, and domination became the norm, society began portraying God using masculine images, as a warrior and ruler.[17] Women became tied to the body and the earth, while patriarchal religion insisted that to be closer to God, one had to transcend both. Holiness required rejecting the physical body and the natural world, creating a theology that justified the domination of women and nature alike. This worldview left women and the earth at the mercy of those who claimed divine authority to rule over them.[18]

Men, associated with intellect, order, and reason, were deemed worthy to rule in the public spheres. Women were associated with nature and seen as wild, unpredictable, and in need of taming. So society sought to domesticate them, relegating women to the private sphere. Rather than beholding the beauty and strength of their power, women's voices were silenced and their wisdom dismissed—pushed to the periphery while men moved freely in spaces of influence and prestige.[19]

As European colonizers claimed land and bodies, women—particularly women of color—were commodified just like the soil they walked on.[20] Both were treated as objects to be exploited for profit and gain.

But the consequences of this erasure extend far beyond symbolism. Around the world, women—especially those in rural and under-resourced communities—bear the weight of environmental degradation in tangible, often devastating ways. Stripped of agency over both their bodies and their lands, they are forced to walk miles for water and firewood while pollution and deforestation deplete the land. Toxic waste dumping and industrial pollution hit poor women the hardest.[21] And when men leave in search of work, it is women who shoulder the sacred responsibilities of nurturing and sustaining their communities. As the natural world continues to be exploited, the burden on marginalized women only grows. This dynamic is what we call the "feminization of poverty," where both women and the earth bear the brunt of exploitative systems and women carry the weight of survival on their backs.[22]

It's not enough to simply critique these systems; we must transform them. Any vision of justice that fails to center women, especially women of color, will always be incomplete. For generations, such women carried an inheritance of wisdom, a knowing that binds the fate of the earth to the faith of their people—nurturing soil and seed, reading the language of ecosystems, and understanding that survival isn't an individual struggle but a collective one.

Across the Global South, women stand at the front lines of resistance against deforestation, against poisoned waters, against a world that treats land and body as things to be consumed. They fight because the earth is kin. Because to safeguard the land is to safeguard the children who play in its fields, the elders who drink from its rivers, the communities that have called it home for generations.[23]

———

In a place they call Cancer Alley—where the land stretches along the Mississippi River between Baton Rouge and New Orleans and the air is thick with the fumes of petrochemical plants—Black women are fighting to save their homes. They walk the land their ancestors tended, a land now marked by industry, breathing air that tastes of metal, drinking water they know isn't safe. But they are not silent. Sharon Lavigne, a teacher turned activist, stands at the forefront. She founded Rise St. James to protect her community from the relentless expansion of chemical plants that bring profit to outsiders but sickness to her people.

Lavigne's fight is not just against toxins; it's against the belief that this land and her community are expendable. She goes door to door, speaking to neighbors about the poisons in their backyard, holds meetings in church basements, marches down roads flanked by towering smokestacks. This is *ecowomanism* in flesh and spirit. She knows that her community's survival is tied to the earth's well-being. Her resistance is an act of devotion, a testament to the resilience of Black women who refuse to let their land—and their people—be consumed. In this place of loss, she has made herself a keeper of life.

Like Sharon Lavigne, women have long risen to defend the land that sustains them. I think of the thousands of Indigenous women in Brazil who stood against Bolsonaro's plans to carve up the Amazon for mining and agriculture. I think of Mamá Tingó, an Afro-Dominican farmer who laid her life down in the fight to protect her people's land from those who saw it only as something to be seized. These women do not just live on the land; they belong to it, the earth itself joining their resistance.

At their heart, movements like ecofeminism—and ecowomanism, which centers Black women and women of color in the struggle for environmental justice—are about reclaiming land, power, and identity. For People of Color, environmental justice is bound to the right to remember the knowledge, the rituals, the ways of tending to the earth that empire tried to strip away. This struggle is not just about policy shifts or legal battles; it's about mending the fractures between body and soil, between memory and belonging, between the land and those who have always known its sacredness.

In her essay "Touching the Earth," feminist scholar bell hooks calls us to reclaim the agricultural wisdom and deep connection to the land that Black communities have carried across the diaspora. This act of remembering is a form of healing and self-determination in the face of white supremacy. "Living close to nature," she writes, "black folks were able to cultivate a spirit of wonder and reverence for life." Tending the earth was not just survival but communion—growing food to sustain the body, flowers to nourish the spirit. To know the land was to know beauty, to witness the sacred in soil and bloom. hooks reminds us that this connection was never lost, only buried, waiting for us to return.[24]

To witness the land with reverence is to enter into a kind of embodied trinity of self, Spirit, and soil. The memories rooted here disrupt the dominant narratives that erase the environmental histories of Black and Brown people. These are stories that live in our bodies, in the hush of wind through the trees, the scent of rain on dry earth. They rise from the deepest parts of who we are, reshaping meaning, reorienting us to the divine.[25] To give voice to the stories of our ancestors is to reclaim what was taken. It is to remember ourselves whole.

Some of my most vivid memories are woven with the breath of the soil. I think of catching tadpoles with my cousin Yetzabel by the lake at her abuela's, the way our hands cupped the tiny creatures like something sacred. I remember the lizard eggs I'd find tucked away at my own abuela's house, how I'd hover over them, guarding them from whatever might come. I think of the ripest aguacates plucked from abuela's tree, their green flesh splitting open under my knife, the taste of them lingering as we sat on the porch in the thick Miami heat, singing Luis Miguel songs into the night. I remember a fourth-grade field trip to Crandon Park, my water shoes sloshing along the shore as I marveled at the tiny crabs wriggling in my net. And I'll never forget the first time I escaped the city lights and gazed up at the symphony of stars in the sky, my back pressed against the sand.

These memories aren't just remnants of childhood—they *make* me. They shape my wonder, my longing, my ache for the divine. The stories of my family's life in el campo of Cuba are a thread running through my very being. My abuela's hands in the soil, tending the land as if it were her own soul, is a memory that holds weight in my bones. When the empire pressed down on her shoulders, the earth rose up in kindness, offering herself to heal the wounds colonialism left behind. And somehow, that sacred exchange of care and healing flows through me too. The earth, like a quiet witness to pain and perseverance, continues to hold and heal us, generation after generation.

I think of the depiction in Revelation 12 of the "sun woman," radiant and crowned, her body a testament to creation itself. She labors to bring forth life, yet a ferocious dragon waits to devour what she bears. Vulnerable yet fierce, she flees to the wilderness after her child is taken to safety, finding a refuge prepared for her. In the wilderness—a sacred space for Israel, a place of both trial and divine encounter—the earth becomes her ally. Like Hagar, who met God in the desolate sands, the sun woman discovers a sanctuary where she can breathe, heal, and be held.

But the dragon's rage doesn't relent. He sends a flood to destroy her, a violent surge symbolic of empire's unchecked force. And in a moment of unexpected agency, the earth herself opens her mouth to swallow the flood, shielding the woman. This is no passive terrain but a living force, wielding her power against empire's violence. It's as if the earth herself is reminding us that she, too, has a voice and the will to protect life.

John, the author of Revelation, tells us that the earth is more than soil and stone. She is an active participant in this cosmic drama, rising to confront death dealing powers and nurture life's resistance. As Brigitte Kahl notes, the earth is responsive and purposeful. She is an interconnected subject who becomes a healer and protector against empire's violence.[26] This story reminds us that the earth is not only our home but also our partner, standing with all who resist.

The earth plays a similar role in the story of Deborah, the prophetess and judge. Guiding Israel in both wisdom and war, Deborah commands Barak into battle against Sisera, the Canaanite oppressor. In the Song of Deborah (Judg. 5), she recounts her triumph, portraying nature as an ally that rises in solidarity.

The earth trembles, rain pours, and mountains quake, rendering Sisera's iron chariots powerless in the mud. Here, the land and the elements are active participants in the liberation of Israel, in partnership with Deborah's leadership. They, too, are entwined in resilience, each embodying a fierce, sacred strength against forces that oppress life.

These images beckon us to see the natural world as a companion in the fight for justice. She too is caught in the struggle between liberation and the suffocating hold of empire. But, as Paul reminds us in Romans 8, creation is on the side of life, longing to heal.

Human consciousness is not superior to the rest of creation but, as scholar Rosemary Radford Ruether calls it, a "gift"—a way to be deeply attuned to the world around us.[27] It invites us not to rise above nature but to descend gently into it, honoring the intricate web that weaves our minds, bodies, and spirits to all living things. This holistic vision challenges systems of hierarchy and domination that insist men must rule over women, humans over animals, able-bodied over disabled. True flourishing is not found in separation and control but in mutuality and interdependence.

Such understanding pulses through many African and Native traditions, where the healing power of the earth extends beyond physical wellness. It is about memory and belonging, about reconnecting with a greater web of life. For the Lakota, the earth reveals the beauty and worth of all beings. Chief Luther Standing Bear once warned, "The old Lakota was wise. He knew that man's heart away from nature becomes hard; he knew the lack of respect for growing, living things soon led to lack of respect for humans too."[28]

In African cosmology, spirit, nature, and humanity are woven together. No act is isolated. To harm the earth is to harm our ancestors, who are believed to dwell within nature. This means that something as simple yet profound as water pollution is not just an environmental crisis but a moral and spiritual one. Water holds memory, and to desecrate it is to disregard the legacy of our elders and the future of our children. There is a sacred relationship between caring for the earth and caring for people.[29] This kind of interdependence pulses at the core of Christian theology.

Many metaphors—eggs, clovers, water in its various forms—have attempted to capture the mystery of the Trinity. And yet, each image falls short, incapable of containing that which is meant to transcend our knowing. The Trinity, like the interconnectedness of earth, spirit, and humanity in African cosmology, whispers a truth too expansive for our language, too mysterious for our metaphors. It is the shape of holy kinship, a communion bound not by hierarchy or power but by an eternal togetherness. The Trinity is a story of belonging, of relationship.

For too long, our interpretations of the Trinity have imagined God in these roles: Father above, the Spirit below, the Son somewhere in between. This hierarchy echoes the world's systems of power, each layer weighing on the next. But the true beauty of the Trinity lies in the absence of such structures. It is an invitation to reimagine God as a relationship based not in dominance but in a belonging vast enough to hold the cosmos.

We, too, are held in this divine embrace, drawn into the life-giving web that stretches from earth to stars. The Spirit moves like wind through trees, like the ocean's tide, reminding us that God's presence is not confined to lofty thrones but is woven into every breath, every grain of sand. There, in the space between Father, Son, and Spirit, is an endless unity, a sanctuary for all life, a love that overflows into the soil, the rivers, the mountains.

In Jesus, we see the depths of this kinship. God becoming flesh and blood, entering the rhythms of earth's seasons and cycles. This embodiment is a call not to rise above creation but to root ourselves within it, as if to say, we belong here, knit into earth's story.

———

The COVID-19 pandemic brought a painful clarity to how deeply connected we all are. Staying home wasn't just about self-preservation; it was about caring for our most vulnerable neighbor. But this interconnectedness runs far deeper than a moment of crisis. The food we eat, the chairs we sit in, the roofs over our heads—all of it is the fruit of someone else's labor and sometimes love as well. Nothing happens in a silo. Martin Luther King Jr. once said, "Before you finish eating your breakfast this morning, you've depended on half the world."[30] His words were meant to serve as a reminder that the fruit we might have eaten today didn't just appear on our plate. Dozens, maybe hundreds of hands touched it before it reached us. Every species on this planet is woven into the same web of life. No thread stands alone.

Yet the rise of individualism, especially in capitalist societies, has made us forget this fundamental truth. As societies moved away from nature and shifted to industrial economies, we were taught that independence is strength and that survival means forging our own paths. Patriarchy amplified these ideas, feeding us the lie that we can be self-reliant, separate from community or creation.[31]

This way of living is unsustainable. To begin healing ourselves and the earth, we must first recognize our deep dependence on this planet. When we do so, we start to see human systems—how we produce, consume, and discard—as part of the larger ecological patterns that sustain all life.[32] The hierarchy we've built between ourselves and nature begins to crumble when we stop trying to dominate her and instead learn at her feet.[33] Take the dandelion, for example. We dismiss it as a weed, but it has the power to heal and detoxify. It flourishes not in isolation but by spreading itself and its community structure. It thrives wherever it finds itself, embodying resilience and connection. As adrienne maree brown says, "A dandelion *is* a community of healers waiting to spread."[34]

To truly address the urgent issues of our time, we must hold the entire family of creation—our ecosystems, our regions, the earth herself—in our hearts. We have to resist the pull of alienation and nihilism.[35] The way back is simple: We must reconnect with the land, stick our hands in the dirt, and begin to love what has been overlooked and unloved for too long.

A Slow, Unstoppable Rebellion

I often wonder when it struck Abuela that she would never return to her island, when that reality of exile set in, the realization that her feet would never again press into Cuban soil. Did the weight of it settle on her chest when she buried her husband across the Atlantic, the vast ocean a reminder of everything she had left behind? As she sprinkled the dirt over his casket, did she imagine it was the same earth that once gave life to her aguacates?

Jeremiah's words to those living under empire come to me as I think of her: build houses, plant gardens, seek peace and well-being, pray (Jer. 29:5–7). There's a kind of holy defiance in pressing seeds into soil, watering them with a gentle, patient hand. Caring for a thing with tenderness in a world that seeks to crush, to suppress, to exploit is resistance—a quiet, rooted kind that refuses to be dislodged by the violence of empire. It's choosing to flourish right where they expect you to wither.

Abuela's calloused hands, worn from years of planting and sowing in her backyard, bore this truth. She grew up in a world that sought to confine her, to tell her who she could be and how far she was allowed to dream. And yet, there she was, every morning, pulling weeds, watering roots, nurturing her garden with a ferocity that felt sacred to me even back then. Abuela's garden was not just a retreat; it was a rebellion.

I once asked her why she cared so much about that little plot of earth. She looked at me with a steady fierceness and said, "Porque nadie me lo puede quitar" (Because no one can take it from me). These blooms, this food—they were a claim to dignity in a world that tried to steal it.

When I was a child, we'd spend hours together, plucking ripe fruit for our afternoon snacks while I heard stories of life in el campo. Her love for her island refused to wane. "Cuba es la isla más bella del mundo" (Cuba is the most beautiful island in the world), she'd remind me often. Seeds were planted in that yard not just to nourish but to keep the memories of her homeland alive. Those trees held stories—of exile, survival, and dreams she refused to surrender.

Jeremiah's exhortation speaks to this. His call to build and plant isn't about submission but about survival. Not bending to empire but growing in spite of it. Because to build a home, to plant food to feed yourself and your children is to say that *I will flourish even here, even while I long for liberation. I will stay human in a world that tries to make me feel anything but.*

This kind of resistance isn't loud or flashy. Instead, it sinks deep into the soil, whispering hope into our homes, into the very fabric of our lives. To "promote the welfare of the city" (Jer. 29:7) is to look at the brokenness of the place where you are planted and say, "I will not turn away. I will not give up." It is to see its wounds and choose to stay with them, to pray for healing while quietly sowing something better right in its midst.

To live this way is to believe that while empires rise and fall, gardens can take root in their ruins.

In Abuela's garden, I felt the weight of this truth. She didn't tend for herself alone. This land became a little ecosystem of care in a community that needed it, a sanctuary where scarcity gave way to abundance.

I remember the last time I walked with Abuela in her garden before her body grew too frail to hold her up. She clutched my arm as we shuffled across the yard to check the mangoes. Her face lit up as she recounted stories, blending memories of Cuba with those of Little Havana. The distinctions didn't matter to her; they were part of the same tapestry.

"¿Sabes que Cuba es la isla más bella del mundo?"

"Sí, yo lo sé" (Yes, I know).

When we reached the tree, she asked me to fetch her old broom to knock down a fruit. I held her steady as she swung with all her might. We laughed when one finally fell, and she picked it up, holding it gently, as though it carried the weight of her story.

We paused by the chain-link fence, and I asked to take her picture. She stood with her mango in hand, a smile soft but radiant. That moment was something holy, as though the earth and her spirit were in perfect communion.

"Vamos a comer" (Let's eat), she said.

Abuela's garden taught me that flourishing doesn't always look like victory. Sometimes it looks like tending a patch of earth, loving it fiercely, and believing in its potential to give life. It's an act of defiance in a world that seeks to commodify and control. Gardens, after all, resist empire in their very being. They nourish without demanding, heal without exploitation, and persist beyond the structures that seek to suppress them.

In the dirt of her garden, I see the truth of Jeremiah's words: to plant, to build, to seek peace is not resignation but resistance. It's declaring that we are not defined by the forces that seek to destroy us. And in the act of tending—soil, relationships, memory—we resist empire's attempts to sever us from the sacred.

So we plant. We build. We tend to one another, believing this living, this rootedness, is resistance too. It's small but profound. It's slow but unstoppable. Our work to love and heal, even in exile, bears witness to a truth bigger than any empire could ever comprehend: We are made for flourishing. No system can strip away our humanity.

Prayer of Resistance

God of Creation,

Forgive our hands that have harmed, for our hearts that have grown distant from the earth's gentle voice. We confess the wounds we've inflicted on the soil and sky, and how we might have let empire disconnect us. In this moment, we remember who we've always been and inhale the healing aroma of the earth—the songs of trees, the wisdom of rivers—restoring us to the beauty of belonging. We are forgiven. We are healed.

We find liberation in our connection to each other, to the earth, and to the divine.

Benediction

May we journey with hands open to give freely and spirits in tune with the heartbeat of the land. May we walk with reverence, side by side with all creatures, honoring the sacred rhythms that pulse through the waters and winds. May our every step echo the ancient song of creation as we live in harmony, guided by love and the quiet wisdom of the land beneath our feet. We rejoice in the abundance of the earth. We commit ourselves to the balance of creation, to sharing, to laughter, and to love.

Amen.

CHAPTER 9

Rejecting Violence, Embracing Peace

Invocation

God of the Cosmos, you who dwell in the vastness and the dust, remind us of our place in a world marked by systems of violence. Uncover in us the roles we play, and open our hearts to the work of unmaking what harms.

We are here to listen, to learn, and to act with compassion and love.

Reflection

The people of Japan tell a story about an old man and a samurai:

In a small village nestled between the mountains, there lived an old farmer named Hiroshi. His community had long been plagued by conflict, feuding with nearby villages over land and resources. One day a powerful samurai rode into the village, he offered to teach the people the art of war so they could protect themselves from future threats. Many villagers

were eager, believing violence would bring peace. But Hiroshi
stepped forward.

"Samurai," he said, "I ask for a day to show you a differ-
ent way." Curious, the samurai agreed.

The next morning Hiroshi invited him to walk through
the rice fields. Together, they saw the stalks bending under
the wind's force but never breaking.

"See how the rice endures by yielding," Hiroshi said. "It
survives not by fighting the storm but by moving with it." At
noon, Hiroshi served tea in silence. The samurai watched as
Hiroshi poured the tea slowly, never rushing, allowing time
for reflection. "True strength lies in stillness, in peace," Hi-
roshi whispered. The samurai, moved by the simplicity and
wisdom of Hiroshi's ways, abandoned his plans of war, real-
izing that peace, like the rice stalk, bends but never breaks.

Those who have ears let them hear.

I can still see myself as a child, marching in line with my
peers, chanting, "I'm in the Lord's army . . . *yes, sir!*" It was
catechism class in the late 1990s, and I was there to prepare
for First Communion. And this is how we did it: by pretending
we were soldiers armed for spiritual battle—the breastplate of
righteousness, the belt of truth, the shield of faith, the helmet of
salvation, the shoes of peace, and the sword of the Spirit. We were
taught that this armor shielded against the devil's schemes. I clung
to these beliefs like a lifeline. Years later, in my evangelical days,
I remained unwavering in my prayers, constantly asking God to
prepare me for war so I might know the peace of Christ—never
noticing the contradiction in my words.

The call to "put on the armor of God" comes from Ephesians 6.
The passage reminds us that our struggle isn't against flesh and

blood but against powers and forces in the unseen realms. What I didn't realize as a child is that this armor was modeled after the gear of Roman soldiers.

Rome's armies, draped in this armor, enforced the Pax Romana (Roman peace), a peace born not of harmony or equality but through forced submission. Historians have called the Pax Romana a "golden age," a time when Rome supposedly flourished. Not only was there "peace" in the empire but also prosperity and security. It was a time of victory, personified by the goddess Victoria, and it came through swords and conquest. Livy, a Roman historian, admitted that for the Romans, war and peace were just two sides of the same coin.[1] Cicero, too, once wrote, "The only reason for waging war is so that we Romans may live in peace."[2] But what is peace if it must be stolen? If it is taken by force, leaving a trail of bodies in its wake? For Rome, peace was never about justice, only the quiet that comes when the oppressed have been silenced.

Empires throughout history—whether Roman, British, or American—have sold us this same idea: that peace is worth any sacrifice, even war, that we can live freely only if someone else is conquered. It's no wonder that Rome's vision of peace infiltrated the language of faith. And yet, central to the Christian story is another vision of peace, one that is unsettling, because it doesn't demand violence to secure it. It's a peace that doesn't need an empire to hold it up.

How do we reconcile these two visions: wearing the armor of Rome while professing faith not in an emperor of violence but in a Prince of Peace?

An emperor was, above all, a man of war. He rose through the ranks as a military general, earning glory with every battle won. Roman men trained for war from a young age, and no one could hold office without first proving themselves on the battlefield. Even as the role of the emperor evolved, the empire itself remained inseparable from the sword, shaping Rome's politics, gods, and very culture.[3] Even ideals like *virtus* (virtue) and *concordia* (harmony) were tied to military success. This belief fueled the myth of *justa causa*—the notion of "just war," which framed Rome's violence as divine mission to bring peace and order to the so-called uncivilized world.[4]

Speaking the Language of Peace

Imperial peace no doubt shaped early Christian beliefs. The letters written to the Ephesians—and also to the Colossians—pulse with imperial language, metaphors, and ideals, cut from the very fabric of Roman rule.[5] Like the rest of the New Testament, their words, their theology, and their vision of ethics and power were shaped by the political and social order of the empire. To read them without acknowledging this entanglement is to miss their depth.[6] Ephesians describes Paul as "an ambassador in chains," as a captured, subjugated apostle just after his call to "put on God's armor" (6:20). It's curious, isn't it? That someone living under the terrorizing rule of Roman power would speak about armor in such a positive light.[7]

It's possible that here, too, the symbols of imperial power are being reshaped, retooled, subverted for a different purpose. Or perhaps this imagery is used simply because it's what's most accessible, like the way John imagines God's kingdom with gates of pearl and streets of pure gold in Revelation, images drawn from the lavish wealth of the elite. For those dreaming of a heavenly world, their imaginations often gravitated toward the grandeur around them. In a similar way, resistance against the empire's brutality in Ephesians is envisioned using the familiar imagery of military armor.

But perhaps there's something deeper. What were once instruments of war suddenly become metaphors for something entirely different: The belt becomes truth, the breastplate becomes justice, the shield becomes faith. Even the sword—the symbol of conquest—is no longer made of steel but of Spirit. When Ephesians speaks of armor, it reimagines violence into a virtue, as if to say, *this empire won't have the final word. Their swords are not sacred. Instead, these are our defenses: truth, justice, peace.*[8]

The call to wear this armor of God is about resisting the "tricks of the devil," which is explained as the powers and rulers that govern this world's darkness. The passage reminds us that our struggle isn't against flesh and blood but against forces in the unseen realms. And these aren't just abstract evils floating in the ether; they are systems, structures, and ideologies designed to uphold the powerful while keeping the rest subjugated. Through this lens, we begin to see how the very symbols of empire are subverted and turned against the forces that wield them.[9]

In the letter to the Colossians, we find a similar defiance: a quiet, profound rebellion hidden in language. For example, the titles given to Christ—such as Lord and Savior—are not mere reverence; they are a direct challenge to the empire's claims of ultimate authority. Words like *salvation*, *gospel*, and *Son of God*, political language once bound to Rome's grip, are redefined with a deeper hope.

The birth of Emperor Augustus was hailed as "good news," the "beginning of all things." He was the "savior of the world," the one who brought harmony and order. Nero, too, was praised for subduing chaos and ushering in an age of prosperity, his rule likened to the gods pacifying the unruly forces of old.[10]

But Colossians dares to say that it is not Augustus, not Caesar, who holds the cosmos together but Christ, who reigns over all creation (Col. 1:17). And in Christ, God's heart for creation is revealed, not through cycles of violence but by a reconciliation that sets creation free.[11]

For Rome, *reconciliation* was the process of dragging the rebellious back into submission, into the "harmony" of the empire. It was a process of reasserting power, ensuring loyalty, and remaking people in Rome's image. The empire's so-called reconciliation came only after its enemies were left with no option but surrender, those conquered bending low to plead for some fragile peace.

But here, reconciliation is not a return to oppression; it is the undoing of it. Where Rome enforces allegiance, Christ draws us into liberation.

It is in these bold declarations that Rome's empty promises are exposed. Roman peace was never truly peace; it was an illusion. While the empire's core may have enjoyed the benefits of war, the margins lived in terror, their lives shaped by poverty and fear. The poor bore the cost, crushed by relentless taxes that drained what little they had. And for those who dared to resist, Pax Romana meant enslavement, devastation, and death. Peace was built on total subservience.

Tacitus, a Roman historian, saw through the illusion, calling out the hypocrisy: "To robbery, butchery, and rapine, [the Romans] give the lying name of 'government'; they create a desolation and call it peace."[12] This narrative is as old as time. The prophet Jeremiah spoke of it when he called out Babylon's violence: "From the least to the greatest, all are greedy for gain; prophets and priests alike, all practice deceit. They dress the wound of my people as though it were not serious. 'Peace, peace,' they say, when there is no peace" (Jer. 8:10–11 NIV).

I imagine this wound. Fresh, red, aching under the weight of what was promised. And yet, those meant to heal it glance over it with a smile and a whisper of peace that barely lingers. We live in a world where those in power will trade in our suffering, package our pain, put out glistening promises like false medicine, just enough to dull us, just enough to make us forget that the wound is still there.

Empire has always had prophets and priests willing to look the other way, to serve comfort instead of justice. They speak of peace to keep things quiet, to keep their kingdoms standing—never mind that the foundation itself is cracked and crumbling under the weight of exploitation, the least of these pressed further down.

This peace is a lie. Real peace, the kind that binds wounds and heals souls, can't coexist with deceit and greed. It isn't handed down from an empire. It's birthed from a fierce love that calls things as they are, that holds the wound up to the light and dares to say, "This cannot stay."

This is the kind of peace the author of Colossians boldly suggests in a dangerous act of subversion. Imperial language is invoked only to be turned on its head. Christ is described as having "brought peace through the blood of his cross" (1:20)—a peace born of reconciliation. One that restores instead of conquers.

I think of Jeremiah's cry, and it feels like an invitation to resist not only empire but the temptation to settle, to soothe without seeing, to pretend that things are as they should be. True peace means bearing witness to the wound and refusing to look away until it heals.

Pax Americana

Empire always finds new names, new narratives to justify itself, new ways to dress war as peace. Like Roman culture, American culture is also steeped in military imagery. The United States built its own version of Pax—*Pax Americana*—on military and economic dominance. From its founding, America has viewed itself as a "new Rome," destined to spread democracy and freedom around the world. It might present itself as a champion of peace, but the reality is the United States maintains military bases in over fifty countries. Its peace is enforced through domination, whether through military interventions or economic control. Pax Americana hinges on a familiar paradox: Its peace is built on imposing its will on others—even and especially through force.[13] In the end, Pax Americana, like Pax Romana, is about who holds power, who benefits from it, and who suffers under it.

Militarism is not just a matter of foreign policy; it is etched into the American imagination. There is a devotion to guns in the United States that feels almost sacred, a faith in warfare as the measure of strength and security. But as Martin Luther King Jr.

173

warned, a country that pours its wealth into military defense while neglecting the flourishing of its people is not simply misguided but inching toward spiritual death.[14]

In this land, there are more guns than people—enough for every man, woman, and child to carry one with millions left over.[15] And the majority of these guns? They belong to civilians. In a nation whose gun laws are the loosest among its peers, this abundance is not without a cost. The United States is a country with 4 percent of the world's population but 35 percent of global firearm suicides, with over 48,000 lives lost to gun violence each year. That's more than 120 people every day, each one held, each one remembered, each one mourned.[16] In 2023, the Gun Violence Archive recorded over 650 mass shootings in the United States.[17] And perhaps most haunting, guns are the leading cause of death for our children.[18] It feels like the earth itself cries out a lament of metal and sorrow held in the bodies of its people. These numbers aren't just data; they're the weight of grief we carry, reminders that we're bound together not just in life but also in loss as we wrestle with the forces that shape this nation's heart. This is a wound we cannot look away from, one we must struggle with until healing comes.

The weight of this grief stretches itself deep into the US justice system, which is yet another example of the way violence often hides behind the veneer of legality and order. Punitive justice in the United States, rooted deeply in retribution, reflects an obsession with control and violence. It aims to impose suffering as payment for wrongdoing yet operates through flawed systems that disproportionately harm marginalized communities. The execution of innocent individuals—like Lena Baker and Carlos DeLuna—stands as a chilling reminder of these failures.[19] Erring in judgment when wielding the irreversible power of life and death is not only a systemic failure but also a theological violation. It reflects a government assuming godlike authority, claiming dominion over who is deemed worthy of life.

This punitive impulse mirrors the American fixation on violence as a means of order and justice, a legacy shaped by empire and conquest. From capital punishment to mass incarceration, the US justice system relies on fear and force, prioritizing punishment over understanding or reconciliation. This approach alienates and dehumanizes, perpetuating cycles of harm rather than breaking them.

Restorative justice offers a radical alternative. It moves beyond retribution, centering healing for both the harmed and the wrongdoer. In place of fear and control, it seeks accountability and transformation, acknowledging the sacredness of every life, even the life of someone who has caused harm. It dares to imagine justice not as violence cloaked in law but as restoration—a collective mending of what empire has broken. In the face of the innocent executed, it asks us to reject fear and embrace the hope of a world where justice nurtures rather than destroys.

The Cross as Shalom

For Rome, justice came in the form of a cross, crafted from wood and nails and utilized as a public humiliation. It was a brutal display of violence meant to intimidate, to demand allegiance through agony, to make an example of those who resisted.

But in Colossians, the cross becomes something entirely different. Here, it's not the conquering power that brings peace and reconciliation but the one *crucified*, the one stretched out on beams meant to symbolize defeat. And in this mystery, what should have signaled utter failure is transformed to the heartbeat of divine harmony. The empire's emblem of death becomes, in Christ, the birthplace of life-giving peace that binds together everything in heaven and on earth. The illusion of Roman peace is unmasked, exposed as a hollow promise, void of true reconciliation.

The message goes deeper. The powers—thrones, dominions, rulers, and authorities that once seemed untouchable, wielding influence over the world as if they have the final say—are nothing more than shadows under Christ's kin-dom, created by and for him (Col. 1:16). In this cosmic reconciliation, these forces are defeated and stripped of their self-appointed authority.

The imagery here is raw and familiar, drawn straight from the Roman *triumphus*—the haunting display of conquered enemies dragged through the streets in chains. The victory parades, designed to etch into memory Rome's sovereignty over life and death, were as much a visual reminder of who held sway over the world as they were a spectacle.[20] Yet Colossians turns this imperial pageant on its head. This victory parade does not center the emperor dragging a procession of captives; rather, Christ's crucifixion is the unexpected triumph in which the imperial powers are disarmed, rendered powerless against Christ's vulnerability and love.

And there's a richer resonance still: Christ, "the head of the body, the church" (Col. 1:18), challenges the whole framework of imperial power. To those first hearing these words, they would recall Caesar, the head of Rome, and Zeus, sovereign over the heavens. But Colossians reshapes power in its entirety. It's not the emperor who embodies ultimate authority; it's Christ, whose power defies the world's expectations. Here is a reign rooted in gentle strength.[21]

When empire used the cross to subdue, Jesus used it to restore. This is restorative justice: healing through relationship and repair. In Christ, justice is not the hammer of empire but the mending of what is broken—the gathering of the lost, the lifting of the fallen, the restoration of dignity where it has been stripped away. The cross does not demand allegiance through fear but invites transformation through love.

And in this sacred reversal, reconciliation finds its true meaning. Enemies are no longer enemies; the estranged are drawn into belonging, woven into a community where love breathes life into existence.[22] Christ's self-giving redefines our very identity, calling us into a peace that heals and binds and makes whole. Here, in the shadow of the cross, we step into divine reality—a place where love transforms empires and grace redraws the boundaries of what it means to belong. Here, we find shalom.

Shalom is not just a simple greeting or the absence of conflict. It's not merely a world where wars have ceased and people just coexist. It is more profound, more ancient. Shalom is the fullness of life, the kind of peace that mends every crack left by sorrow, every fracture carved by violence.

This peace extends to all of creation. The land, the sky, the creatures, and the waters are all part of it, flourishing together. Imagine a world where the earth isn't stripped bare by greed, where the poor no longer hunger and the oppressed no longer cry out beneath the weight of their chains. Shalom is the sound of the earth when it is whole.

And yet, shalom is not passive. It confronts injustice with courage. It insists on healing broken relationships between people, between nations, between humanity and the rest of creation. And it doesn't settle for an easy truce. Shalom calls for repair, for the mending of the torn places in our world, the healing of wounds both seen and unseen. Picture the Jubilee year in ancient Israel, when debts were forgiven and land was returned to its original owners. This wasn't just economic relief; it was an act of justice, a declaration that no one should be trapped in cycles of poverty, that land and life belong to all.

Shalom is the inheritance of those who carried the weight of empire on their backs and still dared to dream beyond it. The prophets, the freedom fighters, the ones who risked everything with the unshakable conviction that this world is not the end of our story did not wait for empire's permission to dream. They believed in a world that could come to life through imagination.

This is where our vision for shalom is grounded. It's a vision that calls us to believe that the truest kind of change comes not from the top down but from the courage and resilience of the people who refuse to be swallowed whole by the systems that bind them. And when we remember them, it is an act of rooting ourselves in a lineage of resistance that empire cannot touch.

Shalom is the peace of all things in their rightful place, where the world hums in the harmony of God's love.[23] It's the kind of peace that exists when nations lay down their swords, lions and lambs rest side by side, and the poor and the powerful share the same table. It's more than restoration; it's renewal—one that calls for a radical rethinking of how we approach strength, vulnerability, and what it means to belong.

We Just Want to Belong

In a world fixated on military might, the image of armor that has shaped our theological imaginations often becomes a reflection of our own fears. Too often, we twist this imagery to teach us how to "guard our hearts" in such a way that makes vulnerability seem like a threat. Told that strength means remaining unshaken, we hide behind walls of self-preservation. But as Brené Brown reminds us, true courage lays down the armor and stands exposed. It is found in the willingness to let ourselves be seen: not just the bright, triumphant parts of our ourselves but the tender, wounded places we keep hidden.[24]

Perhaps this is the truest resistance to empire, the one we must first cultivate within ourselves—to choose vulnerability over violence, peace over power, love over fear. When we begin to strip away our defenses, to dismantle the internal forces that demand control and domination, we make space for the peace of Christ. We make room to become whole. Only in this unarmored honesty can we finally draw near to ourselves, to each other, and to the God who sees us fully.

Beyond theology or belief, it's the hope of belonging to a community that draws many to church. It's what has drawn me. But true belonging—real communion—requires us to show up as we are: imperfect, frayed, and unpolished. And how hard that can be in a place where striving for perfection hums beneath every song and sermon, where we've been trained since childhood to put on emotional armor, to be proud of it, to even see it as holy. We marched and sang of sacred wars and devils, believing our strength was in the armor itself.

But what if the armor keeps us from the very thing we desire most? Because there is power in our words, in our beliefs, more than we know. And when we choose the armor of invulnerability, we may find ourselves walled off from the love and the intimacy we ache for. We protect ourselves right out of the belonging we seek, the deep ache in our bones to be woven into something greater. Brown says this is a longing so primal that we bend ourselves to fit, chasing the approval and validation of others. But fitting in is not belonging; it is a mask, an illusion that keeps us from the very connection our souls hunger for. True belonging is being seen as we are—unhidden.[25]

Social psychologist Geoffrey Cohen explains that social exclusion triggers the same neural pathways in our brains as physical pain. This "social pain," as psychologists have labeled it, courses through us, bearing a weight upon our bodies. Just as hunger or thirst drives us to seek what sustains, so too does this pain. It compels us toward others and toward healing. We crave belonging as if our survival depends on it, because in many ways it does.[26] Loneliness isn't just an ache of the soul. It seeps into the body, gnawing away at health. Studies show that chronic isolation is as dangerous as smoking a pack of cigarettes each day.[27] This tells us what we already know in our bones: Belonging is more than a feeling. It's the lifeline of our very well-being.

Our greatest biological strength as a species has always been our ability to come together, to collaborate, and to weave ourselves into one another's lives and stories. Our humanity is intertwined with our sense of connection, which is why belonging makes us feel included, protected, and valued.[28] Civil rights leader Ruby Sales reminds us that empire erodes intimacy; it severs the ties that bind us, destroying how we relate to and understand one another. The Black community has borne this harm since enslavement. When families were ripped apart, tenderness and intimacy had to be fiercely defended, becoming both weapon and refuge.[29]

Research shows that when we sense our belonging is threatened, when it is at risk for even a moment, something inside us recoils. We retreat into self-preservation, akin to a fight-or-flight response. This causes us to move through the world differently, to act in ways or believe in things we normally wouldn't—betraying our true selves to grasp at some semblance of acceptance. We are so made for belonging that the hunger for it can strip us of our authenticity. But when we are embraced in true belonging, it roots us. It strengthens our ability to be gentle—more compassionate and humane—not only with ourselves but also with the people around us.[30] Our ancestors knew this. For them, belonging wasn't a luxury but a lifeline. They understood that survival was held in the hands of the collective, dependent on how strong and bonded their group was. Community meant protection, nourishment, life.[31] And in its purest form, belonging is not about molding ourselves to fit in; it's about being truly seen and accepted. It is trusting that we are safe in the gaze of another.

I think of the moment Jesus said, "Give to Caesar what belongs to Caesar and to God what belongs to God" (Matt. 22:21). It may sound like Jesus is endorsing compliance and obedience to empire, but what if it's actually a subtle, profound resistance—a reminder of where our truest belonging lies?

Caesar's image stamped onto coins spoke of control, of empire's power to claim what people could see and touch. "Give to God what belongs to God," Jesus says, reminding people that they, too, bear an image—the image of the divine. Neither coins nor empires bear divinity in their bones. But each of us does. We carry a holy mark that no oppressive power can take.

Perhaps, then, in that moment, Jesus wasn't just speaking of tax payments but undermining Rome's entire claim over their lives, showing them that no empire—neither Rome nor any machine of domination—had ultimate authority over who they were. Caesar could claim coins, but he couldn't claim them. Belonging to God, we are a people no empire can possess.

———————

In the empire's world, belonging was a double-edged blade. To be counted, to have a name that meant anything beyond yourself, you had to be willing to shed your own skin, to carve yourself into a shape that mirrored the empire's desires.[32] Conformity to the empire's will was a way of survival, a bitter peace won through the erasure of identity. There was no space for wild diversity, no room for the vast and beautiful spectrum of human existence.

But then this voice, this gospel, cuts through the air: "There is neither Greek nor Jew, circumcised nor uncircumcised, barbarian, Scythian, slave nor free . . ." (Col. 3:11). These labels—Greek, Jew, slave, free—were more than words; they were walls built around souls, barriers defining who could rise, who was condemned to serve. But with Colossians' bold proclamation, the empire's iron categories tremble. In Christ, even the outsider is welcomed. No longer must anyone bow to belong; this new kin-dom dismantles the lie that peace requires our silence.

For those hearing these words, the term *barbarian* would have hit with an edge, summoning images of violence and exile. To Rome, barbarians—especially the Scythians—were beasts, their names whispered in disgust, their bodies exploited in the empire's bloodied arenas. The Scythians were imagined as creatures beyond civility, far from the reach of Rome's supposed light. Roman art, full of boasting, depicted barbarians groveling at the feet of the emperor, a twisted mockery of kinship.

But the way of Jesus stands in stark contrast. This gospel takes the empire's most despised and remakes them, offering not only belonging but belovedness. The reach of Christ's love goes to the most forsaken corners of the imagination and brings forth kin.[33] Here, we find a love that turns the feared into family.

In this new kin-dom, there is no lower rank, no conquest hiding under the guise of unity. Jew and Greek, slave and free, barbarian and Scythian all gather at the same table, each honored as they are. This early Christian community embodied a radical inclusion, in which diverse peoples were brought together through a love that made space for new social and economic possibilities.

When Colossians speaks of putting off the old self, of shedding the garments of empire, it calls us into a transformation that is not about adornment but about a fundamental rebirth. In Roman triumphs, victors would strip away their old clothes and don the robes of victory in a ceremony that celebrated the rule of the conqueror.[34] In the empire, proper dress symbolized civilization itself. To be Roman was to be clothed rightly, while those deemed "barbarians" were marked by their supposed lack of refinement, cast as outsiders not just by geography but by appearance, by dress, by body. This belief endured through European colonization and still lingers into our modern minds. To belong in the empire is to dress the part. But the gospel invites us to clothe ourselves instead in compassion, kindness, humility, gentleness, patience, and above all love. This love is no shallow thing—it binds us, mends us, forms a communion where there were once only categories. In this kin-dom, power falls away, and what's left is a peace so deep that it becomes home, a place where difference can finally breathe. A place of communion, solidarity, and friendship.

When Friendship Becomes Revolution

It is a wild thing to be called a friend of God. Scandalous, even. The one who set the stars in their courses, who could have chosen power and distance, instead moves toward us—not as a ruler demanding submission, not as an overseer measuring our worth, but as a friend. "I no longer call you servants, because a servant does not know his master's business. Instead, I have called you friends" (John 15:15).

Empire does not deal in friendship. It thrives on isolation. Its dominion is built not only through conquest but through the slow separation of people from one another, from themselves, from the earth. It is in the way a body becomes untethered from its own history, in the way a community is fractured, the way an individual becomes convinced they are meant to withstand alone what was always meant to be carried together. If an empire cannot make you silent, it will make you believe that your voice is meant only for yourself.

It is in this isolation that empire names us by our usefulness, our obedience, our silence. It convinces the worker that their labor is their only worth, convinces the oppressed that they suffer alone, convinces the faithful that the divine is too far away to touch. It teaches us that intimacy is reserved for the deserving. Empire relies on secrecy, on obscuring the truth, on keeping the people from knowing the business of the master.

But here is Jesus, disrupting it all. He calls us friend not because we have proven ourselves, not because we have performed well enough to belong, but because love is not transaction. Love is presence. Jesus whispers the business of the master into the ears of fishermen and tax collectors, women and laborers, the weary and the overlooked. He is speaking in parables that make the lowly wise and the wise confused. He is unsettling the world's arrangements, replacing allegiance with affection, duty with desire. He is taking those the world has called servant and calling them beloved.

And once the people know this—that they are no longer servants but friends—empire loses its grip. Because friendship, true friendship, is the death of empire. It cannot be controlled or rationed out in wages or traded in the marketplace. It exists beyond the grasp of power.

I think of the time in Gethsemane, when Jesus, knowing what is to come, does not walk into suffering alone. He does not retreat into isolation, as empire so often teaches us to do—bearing our burdens quietly, making our grief small enough to be palatable to the world. Instead, he brings his friends with him. *Stay with me. Watch with me.* It is not a command, but a plea. A longing for nearness, for presence, for the kind of companionship that does not erase suffering but makes it bearable.

And on the cross, when his body is breaking, he looks down and sees his mother and his friend John. *Behold your son. Behold your mother.* Even in death, he is forging connection, refusing the isolation that empire demands.

In Jesus, we see that friendship is not about convenience or comfort: "Greater love has no one than this: to lay down one's life for one's friends" (John 15:13 NIV). It is about sacrifice, about giving of ourselves in a way that reveals the nature of God's love: reckless, radical, and rooted in grace. This is not a love that is easy; it's the messiness of forgiveness, the vulnerability of admitting our need for each other, and the courage to hold space for another when their world is falling apart. In Colossians, we're told to bear with one another, forgiving as the Lord has forgiven us (3:13). This *bearing with* is the refusal to abandon when things get hard, the stubborn insistence that the love of God is enough to hold us together even when everything else seems to be pulling us apart.

Friendship is about mutual knowing, an exchange of trust that strips away hierarchy. In friendship, we become equals in our shared humanity, each of us flawed, each of us holy. It's a divine leveling that sees the other not as a means to an end but instead as a reflection of the sacred.

This friendship stretches beyond borders, beyond walls, beyond the false divisions that empire tries to erect. In Christ, we see each other not through the lens of power or privilege but through the lens of belovedness.

And yet, in a paradoxical way, friendship isn't just about those grand moments of laying down our lives. Sometimes it's about showing up with tea when we know words will fail. Sometimes it's about sitting with the silence of someone else's grief and not rushing to fill it. It's about calling each other back to life when despair seems too heavy to bear alone. It's about remembering that we are, in the truest sense, bound to one another by a love that does not demand perfection but welcomes the full humanity of the other.

Friendship is where we learn to bend toward each other's wounds with gentleness, where we create a space for reconciliation—not as a performance but as a holy rhythm of grace. And in this, friendship becomes a practice of communion. It is where we taste the nearness of God in the nearness of another. In a world that often feels fragmented, friendship calls us to a belonging that celebrates the sacred diversity of God's creation. It means choosing to see the sacred in those we might otherwise overlook, to offer the hand of friendship to those whom society has pushed to the margins.

The work of friendship means seeing and being seen, loving and being loved, laying down our lives not in grand gestures but in the everyday moments of grace and truth that shape our days. It is here, in this sacred practice of friendship, that we learn what it means to belong to each other and to God. And in this belonging, we catch glimpses of a kin-dom where love has the final word and we are all bound together in the heart of God.

———

I think often of salt. Of how something so ordinary, so elemental became the center of a quiet revolution. In 1930, Gandhi walked 240 miles to the Arabian Sea, accompanied by a small group of followers, to collect salt from the ocean. His act was simple and deliberate, a defiance against British colonial rule and self-appointed overlords who had imposed a tax on salt, making it illegal for Indians to produce their own.

As I imagine him walking, I think of the burden carried by the people he represented—those who had been told they were powerless, dependent, voiceless in their own land. The British Empire wanted control, not just of their resources but of their bodies, their movements, their breath. It was violence dressed as order, as governance.

But Gandhi didn't meet this violence with more violence. Instead, he chose something that must have seemed foolish to the powers that be: salt. He chose the elemental over the exceptional, the steady rhythm of a march over the chaos of battle. What Gandhi knew, what perhaps we all know somewhere deep inside, is that true peace comes when we find the courage to claim what was always ours, without needing to destroy in the process.

On the day he bent down to gather the salt, he wasn't reclaiming just a mineral. He was reclaiming the humanity of a people who had been told that they were nothing more than subjects of an empire. But here's where the quiet magic unfolded: Thousands around the country followed his lead, gathering salt together in subtle rebellion. And with each grain, they refused the narrative that insists violence is the only way to keep peace.

The act wasn't dramatic. The empire didn't collapse overnight. But the power of that moment was undeniable. Peace doesn't always shout. Sometimes it's in the quiet defiance—the simple act of a collective people refusing to participate in violence—that people are set free.

It makes me wonder, how often have we been taught to fight for peace when what we really need is to walk toward it, together, hand in hand?

Prayer of Resistance

Prince of Peace,

We confess the ways we have turned away from peace, the times we've chosen silence when justice called. Forgive us, O Beloved, for forgetting our belonging—for thinking we are not enough, for thinking we are alone. Grant us the courage to embrace one another, to walk toward the peace that makes space for all. Let our hearts beat with the rhythm of unity, for in your peace, we find our true home.

We reject the violence of empire and embrace the peace of Christ.

Benediction

May we be filled with a strength that rises not from the clash of arms but from quiet courage. Let us hold the weight of love like an offering, knowing that true power lies in the gentle persistence to heal, to soften, to mend what has been broken. In the tender pursuit of peace, we find the resilience to endure, to breathe, and to be.

Amen.

A Benediction of Belonging

Invocation

We call upon you, O God, to remind us that kinship is the soil of our humanity. Whether we are weary or full of joy; whether we carry a quiet sorrow in our bones or if we already know a peace that holds us in the night, may we remember that in belonging we find roots that steady us. There is no need to be something other than what we are. May we find the courage to bring our full selves, without demand for change or improvement. May we be as honest with one another as we long to be. May we let go of shame and lean into tenderness so that our bodies and minds can find rest. Help us believe that we are loved, wholly and without condition, that we belong as we are—even if we can't believe that yet.

Prayer of Confession and Release

God of Gentle Understanding,

We confess that we have allowed ourselves to believe we are unworthy of belonging. We confess that we have, at times, created places of exclusion rather than embrace; we have chosen self-preservation over shared presence. Help us see that we are already worthy. We release the weight of needing to be anything other than beloved. May we come home to our belonging in you and in each other.

Reading of Affirmation

From the words of the psalmist:

> I praise you because I am fearfully and wonderfully made;
>   your works are wonderful,
> I know that full well.
>
> —Psalm 139:14 NIV

And from the words of Jesus:

> Come to me, all you who are weary and burdened, and I will give you rest.
>
> —Matthew 11:28 NIV

Reflection on Belonging

Belonging is not a thing we earn; it is a gift given freely, an inheritance from a God who loves without condition. We are not made to be perfect; we are made to be whole. We are not made to hide; we are made to be seen.

Imagine the spaces in your life where you have felt most known, most held, most free. Imagine a place where you were allowed to be fully yourself.

This is a glimpse of what it means to belong to each other and to God.

Take some time now for personal reflection.

Blessing of the Body and Spirit

> In this moment, let us bless our own bodies,
> these carriers of memory, these vessels of longing,
> these forms that hold us and give us voice.

(Hand on heart or head)
I bless my mind, where thoughts scatter and gather,
a home for ideas, dreams, and fears.

(Hand on chest or stomach)
I bless my heart, the center of breath and feeling
where love swells and sorrow finds shelter.

(Hands on arms or legs)
I bless my limbs, these gifts that move and stretch,
that carry me through this world with strength and grace.

Belonging is not just for our minds or spirits; it is for our
bodies as well. We are made in love, every cell and every scar.
May we bless and honor these bodies we have been given.

Prayer of Resistance

May the spaces we inhabit be a sanctuary for all, places where we
lay down pretense and practice honesty. May the life we lead draw
us closer to the heart of God and nearer to the truth of who we are.
May we practice gentleness with ourselves and others, honoring
the stories we carry and the needs we hold. May our longing for
belonging be met in glimpses of the deeper belonging we already
have in the heart of God.

May we create a circle of belonging that includes all.

Benediction

May we go forth knowing that we are woven into a tapestry of
kinship that stretches wide and far, into this world and beyond.
May we carry this knowledge into every place we inhabit, every
moment we breathe. When we feel ourselves shrinking, may we
remember that we belong in all spaces, in all ways. We are loved
not for what we do but for who we are. We are seen, and it is good.

Amen.

Notes

Chapter 1 Rejecting Empire, Embracing Joy

1. "Christ in the Rubble: A Liturgy of Lament," posted December 23, 2023, by Red Letter Christians, YouTube, 31:25–32:18, https://youtu.be/qbHzqU3ZdTs.

2. See Steven Seidman, *Contested Knowledge: Social Theory Today* (Wiley Blackwell, 2016), 271.

3. Seidman, *Contested Knowledge*, 282.

4. Edward Said, *Culture and Imperialism* (Knopf, 1993), 7.

5. Ezra Klein, host, *The Ezra Klein Show*, podcast, "The Sermons I Needed to Hear Right Now," November 17, 2023, https://www.nytimes.com/2023/11/17/opinion/ezra-klein-podcast-sharon-brous.html.

6. Klein, "The Sermons I Needed to Hear Right Now."

7. R. S. Sugirtharajah, *Postcolonial Criticism and Biblical Interpretation* (Oxford University Press, 2002), 102.

8. Jeremy Punt, "Negotiating Empires: Then and Now," in *Studying Paul's Letters: Contemporary Perspectives and Methods*, ed. Joseph A. Marchal (Fortress, 2012), 192.

9. Mitri Raheb, *Faith in the Face of Empire: The Bible Through Palestinian Eyes* (Orbis Books, 2014), 5.

10. Philip Davies, *Memories of Ancient Israel* (Westminster, 2008), 11.

11. Richard Horsley, "Submerged Biblical Histories and Imperial Biblical Studies," in *The Postcolonial Bible*, ed. R. S. Sugirtharajah (Sheffield Academic, 1998), 154–55.

12. Adam Winn, ed., *An Introduction to Empire in the New Testament* (SBL, 2016), 1.

13. Stephen Howe, *Empire: A Very Short Introduction* (Oxford University Press, 2002), 11.

14. Stephen Moore, "The Revelation to John," in *A Postcolonial Commentary on the New Testament Writings*, ed. Fernando F. Segovia and R. S. Sugirtharajah (T&T Clark, 2009), 437.

15. Fritz Farrow and Kelsey Walsh, "Trump Says US Will 'Take Over' Gaza: 'We'll Own It,'" ABC News, February 4, 2025, https://abcnews.go.com/Politics /trump-palestinians-leave-gaza-us-rebuild/story?id=118463249.

16. Musa W. Dube, "Reading for Decolonization (John 4:1–42)," in *John and Postcolonialism: Travel, Space and Power*, ed. Musa W. Dube and Jeffrey L. Staley, Bible and Postcolonialism (Sheffield Academic, 2002), 51–52.

17. Howe, *Empire*, 22–23.

18. Howe, *Empire*, 26.

Chapter 2 Rejecting Lies, Embracing Reality

1. Brené Brown, *Daring Greatly: How the Courage to Be Vulnerable Transforms the Way We Live, Love, Parent, and Lead* (Gotham Books, 2012), 108.

2. Pete Enns, "Snakes Can't Talk: What a Six-Year-Old's Faith Crisis Taught Me About Self-Deception," Odds and Enns, September 20, 2023, https://peteenns .substack.com/p/snakes-cant-talk.

3. Jia Tolentino, *Trick Mirror: Reflections on Self-Delusion* (Random House, 2019), 14.

4. Peter F. Drucker, "Management's New Paradigms," *Forbes*, October 5, 1998, https://www.forbes.com/global/1998/1005/0113052a.html.

5. See David Eagle, "Historicizing the Megachurch," *Journal of Social History* 48, no. 3 (2015): 1–3, https://doi.org/10.1093/jsh/shu109.

6. Katelyn Beaty, *Celebrities for Jesus: How Personas, Platforms, and Profits Are Hurting the Church* (Brazos, 2022), 11.

7. Becca Wood, "Olympics Opening Ceremony Tableau Sparks Controversy Among Christian Community," *Today*, July 27, 2024, https://www.today.com/news /paris-olympics/olympics-opening-ceremony-last-supper-controversy-rcna163929; The Olympic Games (@Olympics), "The interpretation of the Greek God Dionysus makes us aware of the absurdity of violence between human beings," X (formerly Twitter), July 26, 2024, https://x.com/Olympics/status/1816929100532945380.

8. Sean Illing interview with Donna Zuckerberg, "Why the Alt-Right Loves Ancient Rome," *Vox*, November 6, 2019, https://www.vox.com/2019/11/6/20919221 /alt-right-history-greece-rome-donna-zuckerberg.

9. Christopher Kelly, *The Roman Empire: A Very Short Introduction* (Oxford University Press, 2016), 11–12.

10. Kelly, *Roman Empire*, 19.

11. See Adam Winne, ed., *An Introduction to Empire in the New Testament* (SBL, 2016), 1–3.

12. Elisabeth Schüssler Fiorenza, *The Power of the Word: Scripture and the Rhetoric of Empire* (Fortress, 2007), 6–7.

13. Stephen D. Moore, *Untold Tales from the Book of Revelation: Sex and Gender, Empire and Ecology* (SBL, 2014), 22.

14. For more on this, including the history of the word and its ties to colonialism, see Alma Zaragoza-Petty, *Chingona: Owning Your Inner Badass for Healing and Justice* (Broadleaf, 2022).

15. Stephen Moore, "The Revelation to John," in *A Postcolonial Commentary on the New Testament Writings*, ed. Fernando F. Segovia and R. S. Sugirtharajah (T&T Clark, 2009), 442.

16. Moore, "Revelation to John," 437.

17. See Audre Lorde, *The Master's Tools Will Never Dismantle the Master's House* (Penguin, 2018).

18. Lynn St. Clair Darden, "A Womanist-Postcolonial Reading of the Samaritan Woman at the Well and Mary Magdalene at the Tomb," in *I Found God in Me*, ed. Mitzi Smith (Cascade Books, 2015), 195.

19. Darden, "Womanist-Postcolonial Reading," 195.

20. Kat Armas, *Sacred Belonging: A 40-Day Devotional on the Liberating Heart of Scripture* (Brazos, 2023), 201.

21. Robert Young, *Postcolonialism: A Very Short Introduction* (Oxford University Press, 2003), 74.

22. Banksy and David Boyle, "The Alternativity," banksy.blog, December 17, 2017, YouTube, 59 min., 12 sec., https://www.youtube.com/watch?v=9JzgVzUaPU4.

23. Banksy and Boyle, "The Alternativity."

Chapter 3 Rejecting Ideology, Embracing Wisdom

1. Homi K. Bhabha, *The Location of Culture* (Routledge, 2004), xi.

2. See Amanda Carpenter, *Gaslighting America: Why We Love It When Trump Lies to Us* (Broadside, 2018).

3. Delia Cai, "Esther Perel Thinks All This Amateur Therapy-Speak Is Just Making Us Lonelier," *Vanity Fair*, June 26, 2023, https://www.vanityfair.com/style/2023/06/esther-perel-amateur-therapy-speak.

4. Kat Armas, *Abuelita Faith: What Women on the Margins Teach Us About Wisdom, Persistence, and Strength* (Brazos, 2021), 1.

5. T. M. Nahanee, *Decolonize First: A Liberating Guide and Workbook for Peeling Back the Layers of Neocolonialism* (Nahanee Creative, 2020). This workbook is available for purchase at https://www.indigenous-inclusion.com/unlearning/p/decolonize-first-workbook.

6. Nahanee, *Decolonize First*.

7. Kaitlin B. Curtice, *Living Resistance: An Indigenous Vision for Seeking Wholeness Every Day* (Brazos, 2023), 54.

8. "What Does Land Restitution Mean and How Does It Relate to the Land Back Movement?," Community-Based Global Learning Collaborative, accessed January 27, 2025, https://www.cbglcollab.org/what-does-land-restitution-mean.

9. "Calls for Justice," in *Reclaiming Power and Place: The Final Report of the National Inquiry into Missing and Murdered Indigenous Women and Girls* (National Inquiry on Missing and Murdered Indigenous Women and Girls, 2019), https://www.mmiwg-ffada.ca/wp-content/uploads/2019/06/Calls_for_Justice.pdf.

10. Willie James Jennings, *After Whiteness: A Theological Education in Belonging* (Eerdmans, 2020), 6.

11. Boaventura de Sousa Santos, *End of the Cognitive Empire: The Coming of Age of the Epistomologies of the South* (Duke University Press, 2018), 6.

12. Boaventura de Sousa Santos, *Epistemologies of the South* (Taylor & Francis Group, 2014), 30.

13. See Ben Sternke, "Spiritual Formation as the Transfer of Tacit Knowledge," Missio Alliance, April 13, 2023, https://www.missioalliance.org/spiritual-formation-as-the-transfer-of-tacit-knowledge.

14. Book Ban Resources, "Total Instances of Book Bans by State, July 2021–June 2023," PEN America, accessed April 16, 2025, https://pen.org/book-bans/book-ban-resources.

15. Bill Ashcroft, Gareth Griffiths, and Helen Tiffin, *The Empire Writes Back: Theory and Practice in Post-Colonial Literatures*, 2nd ed. (Routledge, 2002), 3–4.

16. Kwok Pui-lan, *Postcolonial Imagination and Feminist Theology* (Westminster John Knox, 2005), 2.

17. M. V. Tlostanova and Walter Mignolo, *Learning to Unlearn: Decolonial Reflections from Eurasia and the Americas* (Ohio State University Press, 2012), 62.

18. Walter Mignolo, "Decolonizing Western Epistemology / Building Decolonial Epistemologies," in *Decolonizing Epistemologies*, ed. Ada María Isasi-Díaz and Eduardo Mendieta (Fordham University Press, 2012), 39–40.

19. David Quint, *Epic and Empire* (Princeton University Press, 1993), 4.

20. Musa W. Dube, *Postcolonial Feminist Interpretation of the Bible* (Chalice, 2000), 115.

21. Musa W. Dube, "'Reading for Decolonization (John 4:1–42)," in *John and Postcolonialism: Travel, Space and Power*, ed. Musa W. Dube and Jeffrey L. Staley, Bible and Postcolonialism (Sheffield Academic, 2002), 215.

22. Jon Berquist, "Postcolonialism and Imperial Motives for Canonization," in *The Postcolonial Biblical Reader*, ed. R. S. Sugirtharajah (Blackwell, 2006), 83–84.

23. Berquist, "Postcolonialism," 92.

24. Pui-lan, *Postcolonial Imagination*, 8–9.

25. Pui-lan, *Postcolonial Imagination*, 9–10.

26. Berquist, "Postcolonialism," 87.

27. Karen King, "Canonization and Marginalization: Mary of Magdala," in *Women's Sacred Scriptures*, ed. Kwok Pui-Lan and Elisabeth Schüssler Fiorenza, Concilium (Orbis Books, 1998), 35.

28. R. S. Sugirtharajah, "Coding and Decoding," in *Postcolonial Criticism and Biblical Interpretation* (Oxford University Press, 2002), 74.

29. See James Clifford, "In the Ecotone: The UC Santa Cruz Campus, Part 3," accessed January 27, 2025, https://people.ucsc.edu/~jcliff/IMAGES/Ecotone3.pdf.

Chapter 4 Rejecting Hierarchy, Embracing Kinship

1. Joe C. Magee and Adam D. Galinsky, "Social Hierarchy: The Self-Reinforcing Nature of Power and Status," *Academy of Management Annals* 2, no. 1 (2008).

2. A. Garner and M. Yogman, "Preventing Childhood Toxic Stress: Partnering with Families and Communities to Promote Relational Health," *Pediatrics* 148, no. 2 (2021), https://doi.org/10.1542/peds.2021-052582; R. A. Lanius, E. Vermetten, and C. Pain, *The Impact of Early Life Trauma on Health and Disease: The Hidden Epidemic* (Cambridge University Press, 2010).

3. Martha Ross, "'Blanket Training': Duggar Family Documentary Shows Harsh Way Babies Taught Obedience," *The Mercury News*, June 6, 2023, https://www.mercurynews.com/2023/06/05/blanket-training-duggar-family-documentary-shows-harsh-way-babies-taught-obedience.

4. Michael and Debi Pearl, *To Train Up a Child* (No Greater Joy Ministries, 1994), 14.

5. Joan E. Durrant, "'I Was Spanked and I'm OK': Examining Thirty Years of Research Evidence on Corporal Punishment," in *Decolonizing Discipline: Children, Corporal Punishment, Christian Theologies, and Reconciliation,* ed. Valerie E. Michaelson and Joan E. Durrant, Perceptions on Truth and Reconciliation (University of Manitoba Press, 2020), 28.

6. Billy Graham, *World Aflame* (Pocket Books, 1965), 23.

7. See Kristin Kobes Du Mez, *Jesus and John Wayne: How White Evangelicals Corrupted a Faith and Fractured a Nation* (Liveright, 2020), 12.

8. Du Mez, *Jesus and John Wayne,* 26.

9. To read more about this, see Krispin and D. L. Mayfield, "Strongwilled: Chapter 3: The Beginnings of the Religious Authoritarian Parenting Movement," Substack, April 22, 2024, https://strongwilled.substack.com/p/chapter-3-the-beginnings-of-the-religious.

10. Du Mez, *Jesus and John Wayne,* 82.

11. Du Mez, *Jesus and John Wayne,* 76.

12. Beth Allison Barr, *The Making of Biblical Womanhood: How the Subjugation of Women Became Gospel Truth* (Brazos, 2021), 34.

13. Adam Winn, ed., *An Introduction to Empire in the New Testament* (SBL, 2016), 10.

14. Winn, *Introduction to Empire,* 9.

15. Bernadette J. Saunders, "Corporal Punishment: The Child's Experience," in Michaelson and Durrant, *Decolonizing Discipline,* 36.

16. Valerie E. Michaelson, "Lies That Have Shaped Us: Racism, Violence, and Ageism in Canadian Churches," in Michaelson and Durrant, *Decolonizing Discipline,* 52–53.

17. "US Indian Boarding School History," The National Native American Boarding School Healing Coalition, accessed February 17, 2025, https://boardingschoolhealing.org/education/us-indian-boarding-school-history/.

18. Anderson Cooper, "Canada's Unmarked Graves: How Residential Schools Carried Out 'Cultural Genocide' Against Indigenous Children," *60 Minutes,* February 12, 2023, https://www.cbsnews.com/news/canada-residential-schools-unmarked-graves-indigenous-children-60-minutes-2023-02-12/.

19. Mark MacDonald, "A Prophetic Call to Churches," in Michaelson and Durrant, *Decolonizing Discipline,* 18.

20. Launch of the Nelson Mandela Children's Fund, Mahlamba'ndlopfu, Pretoria South Africa, May 8, 1995, South African History Online, accessed October 21, 2015, https://www.sahistory.org.za/archive/speech-president-nelson-mandela-launch-nelson-mandela-childrens-fund-mahlambandlopfu-pretori.

21. MacDonald, "Prophetic Call to Churches in Canada," in Michaelson and Durrant, *Decolonizing Discipline,* 22.

22. Margaret Y. MacDonald, *The Power of Children: The Construction of Christian Families in the Greco-Roman World* (Baylor University Press, 2014), 8.

23. Lisa Sharon Harper, *The Very Good Gospel: How Everything Wrong Can Be Made Right* (WaterBrook, 2016), 147–48.

24. Jemar Tisby, *The Color of Compromise: The Truth About the American Church's Complicity in Racism* (Zondervan, 2019), 27.

25. Tisby, *Color of Compromise,* 39.

26. Rachel Held Evans, "Aristotle vs. Jesus: What Makes the New Testament Household Codes Different," August 28, 2013, https://rachelheldevans.com/blog /aristotle-vs-jesus-what-makes-the-new-testament-household-codes-different.

27. Robert Paul Seesengood, "Wrestling with the 'Macedonian Call': Paul, Pauline Scholarship, and Nineteenth-Century Colonial Missions," in *The Colonized Apostle: Paul Through Postcolonial Eyes*, ed. Christopher D. Stanley (Fortress, 2011), 201.

28. Seesengood, "Wrestling with the 'Macedonian Call,'" 201.

29. Seesengood, "Wrestling with the 'Macedonian Call,'" 202.

30. Seesengood, "Wrestling with the 'Macedonian Call,'" 202.

31. Seesengood, "Wrestling with the 'Macedonian Call,'" 203.

32. Seesengood, "Wrestling with the 'Macedonian Call,'" 204.

33. See Olivia B. Waxman, "Breaking Down the Controversy over Florida's New Slavery Curriculum," *Time*, July 28, 2023, time.com/6299290/florida -slavery-curriculum-college-board-controversy.

34. Kat Armas, *Sacred Belonging: A 40-Day Devotional on the Liberating Heart of Scripture* (Brazos, 2023), 184.

35. Ada María Isasi-Díaz, *Mujerista Theology: A Theology for the Twenty-First Century* (Orbis Books, 1996), 65–66.

36. Daniel J. Siegel and Tina Payne Bryson, *The Whole-Brain Child: 12 Revolutionary Strategies to Nurture Your Child's Developing Mind* (Delacorte, 2011).

37. "News Release: Upper Sioux Community and State of Minnesota Mark the Return of Sacred Land," Department of Natural Resources, March 15, 2024, https://www.dnr.state.mn.us/news/2024/03/15/upper-sioux-community-and-state -minnesota-mark-return-sacred-land.

38. Brené Brown, *Atlas of the Heart: Mapping Meaningful Connection and the Language of Human Experience* (Random House, 2021), 154.

Chapter 5 Rejecting Dualism, Embracing Paradox

1. On Plato, see Randy Woodley, *Mission and the Cultural Other* (Cascade Books, 2002), chap 9.

2. Marimba Ani, *Yurugu: An African-Centered Critique of European Cultural Thought and Behavior* (African World, 1994), 30.

3. See discussion in Gillian McCulloch, *The Deconstruction of Dualism in Theology: With Special Reference to Ecofeminist Theology and New Age Spirituality*, Paternoster Biblical and Theological Monographs (Paternoster, 2002), 13.

4. Terrence E. Cook, "'Misbegotten Males?' Innate Differences and Stratified Choice in the Subjection of Women," *Western Political Quarterly* 36, no. 2 (1983): 194–220.

5. McCulloch, *Deconstruction of Dualism*, 22–23.

6. See Oscar García-Johnson, *Spirit Outside the Gate: Decolonial Pneumatologies of the American Global South*, Missiological Engagements (IVP Academic, 2019), 59.

7. García-Johnson, *Spirit Outside the Gate*, 59.

8. McCulloch, *Deconstruction of Dualism*, 9.

9. Megan K. Westra, *Born Again and Again: Jesus' Call to Radical Transformation* (Herald, 2020), 31.

10. Westra, *Born Again and Again*, 32.

11. Amos Yong, "'The Light Shines in the Darkness': Johannine Dualism and the Challenge for Christian Theology of Religions Today," *Journal of Religion* 89, no. 1 (2009): 34.

12. See Frantz Fanon, *Black Skin, White Masks* (Grove Press, 1967).

13. Homi K. Bhabha, *The Location of Culture* (Routledge, 2004), 122.

14. Bhabha, *Location of Culture*, 129–31.

15. See P. P. Li, "Toward a Geocentric Framework of Trust: An Application to Organizational Trust," *Management and Organization Review* 4, no. 3 (2008): 416.

16. Richard Rohr, *Falling Upward: A Spirituality for the Two Halves of Life* (Wiley & Sons, 2011), 133.

17. Rohr, *Falling Upward*, 151.

18. Shannan Martin (@shannanwrites), "I was walking through receiving at work," Instagram, December 10, 2024, https://www.instagram.com/p/DDaxZuNpgQ1/.

Chapter 6 Rejecting Hustle, Embracing Slowness

1. See Sonya Marie Taylor, *The Body Is Not an Apology: The Power of Radical Self-Love*, 2nd ed. (Berrett-Koehler, 2021), 43.

2. Taylor, *The Body Is Not an Apology*, 7–8.

3. Kris Manjapra, *Colonialism in Global Perspective* (Cambridge University Press, 2020), 201–2.

4. Camila Domonoske, "'Father of Gynecology,' Who Experimented on Slaves, No Longer on Pedestal in NYC," NPR, April 17, 2018, https://www.npr.org/sections/thetwo-way/2018/04/17/603163394/-father-of-gynecology-who-experimented-on-slaves-no-longer-on-pedestal-in-nyc.

5. Manjapra, *Colonialism in Global Perspective*, 212.

6. Elizabeth Staszak, "'Blessed Are the Poor in Spirit': Disability as a Blessing, Ableism as a Curse," Substack, July 31, 2024, https://staszak.substack.com/p/blessed-are-the-poor-in-spirit-disability.

7. This is a working definition by Talila A. Lewis. See her article "Longmore Lecture: Context, Clarity, and Grounding," Talila A. Lewis (blog), March 5, 2019, https://www.talilalewis.com/blog/longmore-lecture-context-clarity-grounding.

8. Marta Russell and Keith Rosenthal, *Capitalism and Disability: Selected Writings by Marta Russell* (Haymarket Books, 2019), 10.

9. Julia Watts Belser, *Loving Our Own Bones: Disability Wisdom and the Spiritual Subversiveness of Knowing Ourselves Whole* (Beacon, 2023), 53.

10. Belser, *Loving Our Own Bones*, 52.

11. Aníbal Quijano, "Coloniality of Power, Eurocentrism, and Latin America," *Nepantla: Views from the South* 1, no. 3 (2000): 217.

12. See James Fulcher, *Capitalism: A Very Short Introduction* (Oxford University Press, 2004), 2.

13. Quijano, "Coloniality of Power," 218.

14. Quijano, "Coloniality of Power," 216.

15. Fulcher, *Capitalism*, 83–85.

16. Russell, *Capitalism and Disability*, 18.

17. Fulcher, *Capitalism*, 14.

18. Fulcher, *Capitalism*, 15.

19. Fulcher, *Capitalism*, 7–8.

20. Fulcher, *Capitalism*, 8–9.

21. Lynn Parramore, "Before Capitalism, Medieval Peasants Got More Vacation Time Than You. Here's Why," Evonomics, November 2, 2016, https://evonomics.com/capitalism-medieval-peasants-got-vacation-time-heres/.

22. Robin Wall Kimmerer, *Braiding Sweetgrass: Indigenous Wisdom, Scientific Knowledge, and the Teachings of Plants* (Milkweed Editions, 2013), 233.

23. Katharina Hunfeld, "The Coloniality of Time in the Global Justice Debate: De-Centering Western Linear Temporality," *Journal of Global Ethics* 18, no. 1 (2022): 104.

24. Hunfeld, "Coloniality of Time," 104.

25. Walter Mignolo, *The Darker Side of Western Modernity: Global Futures, Decolonial Options* (Duke University Press, 2011), 152.

26. Rolando Vazquez, "Modernity, Coloniality, and Visibility: The Politics of Time," *Sociological Research Online* 14, no. 4 (2009): 3.

27. Krista Tippett interview with John O'Donohue, "John O'Donohue: The Inner Landscape of Beauty," *On Being with Krista Tippett*, February 28, 2008, https://onbeing.org/programs/john-odonohue-the-inner-landscape-of-beauty/.

28. Jon Bloom, "Come, All Who Are Weary," Desiring God, May 13, 2016, https://www.desiringgod.org/articles/come-all-who-are-weary.

29. Belser, *Loving Our Own Bones*, 53.

30. Taylor, *The Body Is Not an Apology*, 9.

31. Taylor, *The Body Is Not an Apology*, 82.

32. Taylor, *The Body Is Not an Apology*, 64.

33. Jia Tolentino, *Trick Mirror: Reflections on Self-Delusion* (Random House, 2019), 80.

34. Taylor, *The Body Is Not an Apology*, 92–93.

Chapter 7 Rejecting Sameness, Embracing Wholeness

1. Blaise Gainey, "House Speaker Threatens Expulsion for Three Lawmakers over Protest Participation," WPLN, April 2, 2023, https://wpln.org/post/house-speaker-threatens-expulsion-for-three-lawmakers-over-protest-participation/.

2. CNN Tonight, Transcripts, April 6, 2023, https://transcripts.cnn.com/show/cton/date/2023-04-06/segment/01.

3. TN House Republicans (@tnhousegop), "Referencing the bipartisan and unanimously approved rules for House decorum and dress attire is far from a racist attack," X (formerly Twitter), February 9, 2023, https://x.com/tnhousegop/status/1623805588525178881.

4. Eric Barreto, "Crafting Colonial Identities: Hybridity and the Roman Empire," in *An Introduction to Empire in the New Testament*, ed. Adam Winn (SBL, 2016), 117.

5. Krista Tippett interview with Luis Alberto Urrea, "Luis Alberto Urrea: On Our Belonging to Each Other," *On Being with Krista Tippett*, July 12, 2018, https://onbeing.org/programs/luis-alberto-urrea-on-our-belonging-to-each-other/.

6. André Munro, "Benedict Anderson," *Encyclopedia Britannica*, May 6, 2024, https://www.britannica.com/biography/Benedict-Anderson.

7. Kwok Pui-lan discusses Winthrop's sermon, delivered in 1630, in *Postcolonial Politics and Theology: Unraveling Empire for a Global World* (Westminster John Knox Press, 2021), 79.

8. Kelly Brown Douglas, *Stand Your Ground: Black Bodies and the Justice of God* (Orbis Books, 2015), 19.

9. Pui-lan, *Postcolonial Politics and Theology*, 79.

10. Willie James Jennings, *The Christian Imagination: Theology and the Origins of Race* (Yale University Press, 2010), 8.

11. Douglas, *Stand Your Ground*, 62–63.

12. Catherine Keller, *God and Power: Counter-Apocalyptic Journeys* (Fortress, 2005), 99–101.

13. Neil Elliott, *The Arrogance of Nations: Reading Romans in the Shadow of Empire* (Fortress Press, 2008), 2.

14. Edwidge Danticat, "The Long Legacy of Occupation in Haiti," *The New Yorker*, July 28, 2015, https://www.newyorker.com/news/news-desk/haiti-us-oc cupation-hundred-year-anniversary.

15. Edward W. Said, *Culture and Imperialism* (Vintage Books, 1993), xii.

16. Said, *Culture and Imperialism*, 13.

17. Robert Paul Seesengood, "Wrestling with the 'Macedonian Call': Paul, Pauline Scholarship, and Nineteenth-Century Colonial Missions," in *The Colonized Apostle: Paul Through Postcolonial Eyes*, ed. Christopher D. Stanley (Fortress, 2011), 191.

18. Seesengood, "Wrestling with the 'Macedonian Call,'" 192.

19. Seesengood, "Wrestling with the 'Macedonian Call,'" 195.

20. Kat Armas, *Sacred Belonging: A 40-Day Devotional on the Liberating Heart of Scripture* (Brazos, 2023), 76–77.

21. Brené Brown, *Atlas of the Heart: Mapping Meaningful Connection and the Language of Human Experience* (Random House, 2021), xxi.

22. Stan Smith, *Poetry and Displacement* (Liverpool University Press, 2007), 124.

23. Bill Ashcroft, Gareth Griffiths, and Helen Tiffin, *The Empire Writes Back: Theory and Practice in Post-Colonial Literatures*, 2nd ed. (Routledge, 2002), 7.

24. Frantz Fanon, *Black Skin, White Masks*, trans. Charles Lam Markmann (Grove, 1967), 16.

25. Walter Mignolo, *Local Histories/Global Designs: Coloniality, Subaltern Knowledges, and Border Thinking*, Princeton Studies in Culture/Power/History (Princeton University Press, 2000), 253.

26. Mignolo, *Local Histories*, 243.

27. See Oscar García-Johnson, *Spirit Outside the Gate: Decolonial Pneumatologies of the American Global South*, Missiological Engagements (IVP Academic, 2019), 271–72.

28. Lisa Sharon Harper, *The Very Good Gospel: How Everything Wrong Can Be Made Right* (WaterBrook, 2016), 142.

29. Walter Brueggemann, *Genesis*, Interpretation: A Bible Commentary for Teaching and Preaching (John Knox, 1982), 100.

Chapter 8 Rejecting Dominance, Embracing Connection

1. A. Malo Larrea, M. Ambrosi de la Cadena, J. Collado Ruano, and L. Gallardo Fierro, "Transcending the Nature-Society Dichotomy: A Dialogue Between the Sumak Kawsay and the Epistemology of Complexity," *Ecological Economics* 216 (2024).

2. Krista Tippett interview with Janine Benyus and Azita Ardakani Walton, "On Nature's Wisdom for Humanity," *On Being with Krista Tippett*, June 6, 2024, https://onbeing.org/programs/janine-benyus-and-azita-ardakani-walton-on-natures-wisdom-for-humanity/.

3. Jeremy Punt, *Postcolonial Biblical Interpretation: Reframing Paul*, Studies in Theology and Religion (Brill, 2015), 196, 203.

4. Barbara R. Rossing, "Alas for the Earth! Lament and Resistance in Revelation 12," in *The Earth Story in the New Testament*, ed. Norman C. Habel and Vicky Balabanski, 5th ed. (Sheffield Academic Press, 2002), 186.

5. Rossing, "Alas for the Earth!," 187.

6. Brigitte Kahl, "Gaia, Polis, and Ekklesia at the Miletus Market Gate: An Eco-Critical Reimagination of Revelation 12:16," in *The First Urban Churches*, vol. 1, *Methodological Foundations*, ed. James R. Harrison and L. L. Welborn (SBL, 2015), 129.

7. Rossing, "Alas for the Earth!," 188.

8. Davina Lopez, "Visualizing Significant Otherness: Reimagining Paul(ine Studies) Through Hybrid Lenses," in *The Colonized Apostle: Paul Through Postcolonial Eyes*, ed. Christopher D. Stanley (Fortress 2011), 83.

9. Lopez, "Visualizing Significant Otherness," 340.

10. Susan Cole, *Power Surge: Sex, Violence, and Pornography* (South End Press, 2000).

11. Jia Tolentino, *Trick Mirror: Reflections on Self-Delusion* (Random House, 2020), 85.

12. Kathryn Miles, "Ecofeminism," Saving Earth / Encyclopedia Britannica, accessed April 16, 2025, https://explore.britannica.com/explore/savingearth/ecofeminism/.

13. Carol J. Adams, *Ecofeminism and the Sacred* (Continuum, 1993), 1.

14. Merlin Stone, *When God Was a Woman* (Harcourt Brace Jovanovich, 1978).

15. Devon Allen, "Mythological Girls: Pachamama," Girl Museum, October 12, 2017, https://www.girlmuseum.org/mythological-girls-pachamama/.

16. Stone, *When God Was a Woman*, xiii.

17. Rosemary Radford Ruether, ed., *Women Healing Earth: Third World Women on Ecology, Feminism, and Religion* (Orbis Books, 1996), 4.

18. Mercedes Canas, "In Us Life Grows," in Ruether, *Women Healing Earth*, 27.

19. Corinne Kumar D'Souza, "Mama Coyote Talks to the Boys," in *Healing the Wounds: The Promise of Ecofeminism*, ed. Judith Plant (New Society Publishers, 1989), 35.

20. Aníbal Quijano and Michael Ennis, "Coloniality of Power, Eurocentrism, and Latin America," *Nepantla: Views from South* 1, no. 3 (2000): 216.

21. Ruether, *Women Healing Earth*, 6.

22. Lin Nelson, "The Place of Women in Polluted Places," in *Reweaving the World: The Emergence of Ecofeminism*, ed. Irene Diamond and Gloria Orenstein (Sierra Club Books, 1990), 184.

23. Nelson, "Place of Women," 185.

24. bell hooks, *Sisters of the Yam: Black Women and Self-Recovery* (South End Press, 2005), 137.

25. Nelson, "Place of Women," 184.

26. Kahl, "Gaia, Polis, and Ekklesia," 115–17.

27. Rosemary Radford Ruether, "Sin, Nature, and Black Women's Bodies," in *Ecofeminism and the Sacred*, ed. Carol J. Adams (New York: Continuum, 1993), 21.

28. Quoted in Llewellyn Vaughan-Lee, ed., *Spiritual Ecology: The Cry of the Earth* (Golden Sufi Center, 2013), 101.

29. Melanie L. Harris, *African American Women and Earth-Honoring Faiths* (Orbis Books, 2017), 17.

30. Martin Luther King Jr. "The Man Who Was a Fool," sermon delivered at the Detroit Council of Churches' Noon Lenten Services, March 6, 1961, https://kinginstitute.stanford.edu/king-papers/documents/man-who-was-fool-sermon-delivered-detroit-council-churches-noon-lenten.

31. Henri C. Santos, Michael E. W. Varnum, and Igor Grossmann, "Global Increases in Individualism," *Psychological Science* 28, no. 9 (2017): 1228–39, https://doi.org/10.1177/0956797617700622.

32. Ruether, "Sin, Nature, and Black Women's Bodies," 21.

33. Sami Brisson, "Women's Connectedness to Nature: An Ecofeminist Exploration," All Regis University Theses, 2017, https://epublications.regis.edu/theses/846/.

34. adrienne maree brown, *Emergent Strategy: Shaping Change, Changing Worlds* (AK Press, 2017), 10.

35. Charlene Spretnak, "Ecofeminism: Our Roots and Flowering," in *Reweaving the World: The Emergence of Ecofeminism*, ed. Irene Diamond and Gloria Orenstein (Sierra Club Books, 1990), 12.

Chapter 9 Rejecting Violence, Embracing Peace

1. Ali Parchami, *Hegemonic Peace and Empire: The Pax Romana, Britannica and Americana* (Routledge, 2009), 19.

2. Christopher Kelly, *The Roman Empire: A Very Short Introduction* (Oxford University Press, 2006), 19.

3. Stephen Howe, *Empire: A Very Short Introduction* (Oxford University Press, 2002), 13.

4. Parchami, *Hegemonic Peace and Empire*, 26.

5. There's no scholarly consensus that Paul wrote Ephesians and Colossians. While they are traditionally attributed to him, critical scholarship has long debated their authorship. Many scholars consider Ephesians to be deutero-Pauline, meaning it was likely written by a follower or admirer of Paul rather than the apostle himself. For sake of clarity, however, I will refer to Paul as the author when referring to this text.

6. Harry Maier, "Colossians, Ephesians, and Empire," in *An Introduction to Empire in the New Testament*, ed. Adam Winn (SBL, 2016), 186.

7. Ekaputra Tupamahu, "Ephesians 6:10–20," *Interpretation: A Journal of Bible and Theology* 76, no. 3 (2022): 251–53.

8. Maier, "Colossians, Ephesians, and Empire," 186–91.

9. Walter Wink, *Naming the Powers: The Language of Power in the New Testament* (Philadelphia: Fortress, 1984), 85.

10. Harry O. Maier, "A Sly Civility: Colossians and Empire," *Journal for the Study of the New Testament* 27, no. 3 (2005): 334, https://doi.org/10.1177/0142064X05052509.

11. Mark S. Medley, "Subversive Song: Imagining Colossians 1:15–20 as a Social Protest Hymn in the Context of Roman Empire," *Review and Expositor* 116, no. 4 (2019): 432.

12. Parchami, *Hegemonic Peace and Empire*, 37.

13. Parchami, *Hegemonic Peace and Empire*, 177, 186.

14. Martin Luther King Jr., "Beyond Vietnam: A Time to Break Silence," speech delivered at Riverside Church, New York City, April 4, 1967, https://www.americanrhetoric.com/speeches/mlkatimetobreaksilence.htm.

15. Christopher Ingraham, "There Are More Guns Than People in the United States, According to a New Study of Global Firearm Ownership," *The Washington Post*, June 19, 2018, https://www.washingtonpost.com/news/wonk/wp/2018/06/19/there-are-more-guns-than-people-in-the-united-states-according-to-a-new-study-of-global-firearm-ownership/.

16. John Gramlich, "What the Data Says About Gun Deaths in the U.S.," Pew Research Center, March 5, 2025, https://www.pewresearch.org/short-reads/2025/03/05/what-the-data-says-about-gun-deaths-in-the-us.

17. Gun Violence Archive, January 8, 2025, https://www.gunviolencearchive.org/.

18. "Statistics," Gifford's Law Center, accessed March 15, 2025, https://giffords.org/lawcenter/gun-violence-statistics/.

19. For information on Lena Baker, see Kathy Lohr, "Georgia Woman Pardoned 60 Years After Her Execution," NPR, August 26, 2025, https://www.npr.org/2005/08/26/4818124/ga-woman-pardoned-60-years-after-her-execution. For information on Carlos DeLuna, see Ed Pilkington, "The Wrong Carlos: How Texas Sent an Innocent Man to His Death," *The Guardian*, May 2012, https://www.theguardian.com/world/2012/may/15/carlos-texas-innocent-man-death.

20. Gordon Zerbe and Muriel Orevillo-Montenegro, "The Letter to the Colossians," in *A Postcolonial Commentary on the New Testament Writings*, ed. Fernando F. Segovia and R. S. Sugirtharajah (T&T Clark, 2009), 299–300.

21. Brian J. Walsh and Sylvia C. Keesmaat, *Colossians Remixed: Subverting the Empire* (IVP Academic, 2004), 90.

22. Maier, "Sly Civility," 340.

23. Walsh and Keesmaat, *Colossians Remixed*, 42.

24. Brené Brown, *Daring Greatly: How the Courage to Be Vulnerable Transforms the Way We Live, Love, Parent, and Lead* (Gotham Books, 2012), 137.

25. Brown, *Daring Greatly*, 145.

26. Geoffrey Cohen, *Belonging: The Science of Creating Connection and Bridging Divides* (Norton, 2022), ix–x.

27. Cohen, *Belonging*, x.

28. Owen Eastwood, *Belonging: The Ancient Code of Togetherness* (Quercus, 2021), 24.

29. Krista Tippett interview with Ruby Sales, "Ruby Sales: Where Does It Hurt?," *On Being with Krista Tippett*, January 16, 2020, https://onbeing.org/programs/ruby-sales-where-does-it-hurt/.

30. Cohen, *Belonging*, ix–x.

31. Eastwood, *Belonging*, 8–9.

32. Eric Barreto, "Crafting Colonial Identities: Hybridity and the Roman Empire," in *An Introduction to Empire in the New Testament*, ed. Adam Winn (SBL, 2016), 117.

33. Maier, "Sly Civility," 343–44.

34. Maier, "Sly Civility," 344.

KAT ARMAS (MDiv, MAT, Fuller Theological Seminary) is a Cuban American writer and podcaster and the recipient of Fuller Seminary's Frederick Buechner Award for Excellence in Writing. She is pursuing a ThM at Vanderbilt Divinity School. Armas is the author of two books, *Abuelita Faith* and *Sacred Belonging.* She has written for *Christianity Today, Sojourners, Relevant,* National Catholic Reporter, Christians for Biblical Equality, Fuller Youth Institute, *Fathom* magazine, and Missio Alliance. Armas lives in middle Tennessee with her family.

Connect with Kat _____

KATARMAS.COM

KATARMAS.SUBSTACK.COM

@KATARMAS

@KAT_ARMAS

@KAT_ARMAS

www.ingramcontent.com/pod-product-compliance
Lightning Source LLC
Chambersburg PA
CBHW021152260326
41798CB00029B/364